T0130024

Reflections on a Life of Jewish Commitment

Essays Honoring Harold Smith in Celebration of His 100th Birthday

May 2018

Edited by
Rabbi Mitchell Smith

authorHOUSE®

AuthorHouse™
1663 Liberty Drive
Bloomington, IN 47403
www.authorhouse.com
Phone: 1 (800) 839-8640

Published by AuthorHouse 05/11/2018

ISBN: 978-1-5462-3921-5 (sc)
ISBN: 978-1-5462-3922-2 (e)

Library of Congress Control Number: 2018904883

Print information available on the last page.

This book is printed on acid-free paper.

Contents

נִבְחָר שֵׁם מֵעֹשֶׁר רָב, מִכֶּסֶף וּמִזָּהָב חֵן טוֹב

A good name is more desirable than great riches; to be held in high esteem is preferable to silver or gold.

Proverbs 22:1

Do not be concerned with what people think of you; for if others can measure you better than you do yourself, you will always be running about to find out what you are. This being dependent on others for one's happiness is the source of all man's infirmities. Only the joy which wells up wholly from within is sound and reliable. It grows and stays with us till the end, while the things that bring approbation of the crowd are evanescent.

Seneca

(Rabbi Tarfon) used to say: It is not your responsibility to finish the work, but neither are you free to abstain from it.

Pirke Avot 2:16

Harold at his 95th birthday party.

חֲנֹךְ לַנַּעַר עַל-פִּי דַרְכּוֹ גַּם כִּי יַזְקִין לֹא יָסוּר מִמֶּנָּה.

Train up a child in the way he should go, and even when he is old, he will not depart from it.

Proverbs 22:6

Jews are the only nation in history to predicate its survival on education. Thanks to Torah, Jews never forgot (that Judaism) is a never-ending effort of education in which parents, teachers, homes and schools are all partners in the dialogue between the generations. Learning – Talmud Torah – is the very foundation of Judaism, the guardian of our heritage and hope. That is why, when tradition conferred on Moses the greatest honor, it did not call him "our hero, "our prophet," or "our king." It called him simply Moshe Rabeinu, Moses our teacher. For it is in the arena of education that the battle for a good society is won or lost.

Rabbi Jonathan Sacks

There was not a Smith to be found in all the Land of Israel.

1 Samuel 13:19

Note on Hebrew usage:

The phrase *zichrono livracha*, meaning "may his memory be for a blessing" (or *zichrona livracha* for a female) is often referenced by the acronym z'l. The Hebrew *alav hashalom* (or *aleha* for a female) is the equivalent of Rest in Peace. It is customary when mentioning two individuals together, one of whom is still living, to add *she-yibadel lechayim arukim*, "may he, by contrast, be granted a long life."

Preface

ALONGSIDE THE NAMES of Leonard Bernstein and Nelson Mandela, giants of the 20th century who would have turned 100 in 2018, one finds other, equally recognizable names like Ted Williams, Rita Hayworth, Sam Walton and Mike Wallace. Among those who *did in fact* make it to that special milestone is our own father, Harold Smith

As the essays in this volume attest to, when it comes to Jewish life in the Twin Cities and beyond, Harold, too, is something of a giant. Together with our mother Mickey, his partner in life of some 67 years, his impact on so many of the Jewish institutions that advance the richness of Jewish life is evidenced in the pages that follow.

Harold's legacy of community service includes tenures as president of the Talmud Torah of St. Paul, president of Hillel at the University of Minnesota, and as a long-time board member of Herzl Camp, to whose inaugural Hall of Fame he was named (together with Mickey) in 2016.

Harold and Mickey took their place as a distinguished couple in local Jewish philanthropy. Their Judaica collection alongside a generous bequest created the Harold and Mickey Smith Gallery of Judaica at the Minneapolis Institute of Arts. While there were those who supported the MIA on a much larger scale, our mother in particular got a kick out of hobnobbing with the likes of MIA Trustee Bruce Dayton at museum functions.

With Mickey's lead, they gave generously to Hadassah, supporting the building of the impressive new Hadassah Medical Center Tower in Jerusalem, and more importantly, spearheading the creation of the Mickey and Harold Smith Enhancement Center on the premises. It was our mother who was the force behind this facility where individuals undergoing chemotherapy can receive critical support and care in their appearance, including high quality human hair wigs and the services of a cosmetician, to counter the harsh effects of their therapies. When our sister Margie, whose life was tragically cut short by her own cancer, sought out a proper wig during her chemotherapy, she was less than thrilled by what was available at the time. The letters which our parents received over the years from Hadassah telling of the immense gratitude of one individual after another who benefitted from this Center, speak of the same concern for the welfare of others that Margie embodied as the "Pearl Mesta" of her group in Washington, D.C.

Harold came by his passionate support for Jewish life naturally, having grown up in the close-knit community of St. Paul's West Side. In close proximity to the Smith residence at 193 E. Robie were numerous cousins and second cousins, a colorful group that included "Maish the Plumber" (aka "Mushma") and "Maish the Druggist" (as they would later be known) and both sets of grandparents, who brought with them their Jewish ways from the so-called Old Country.

We can still remember the Children's Illustrated edition of the Bible, whose stories our father would read to the three of us each night at our home on Highland Parkway, followed by recitation of the *Shma*. The ultimate value of this nightly ritual is underscored by Rabbi Alexander Davis, who notes in this volume how, at some point, Jews "outsourced our studies from parents to teachers, from home to school. The *Sh'ma* got it right - learning begins at home, *b'shivtekha b'veitekha*." We got that from Harold in full measure.

Friday night services at the Temple of Aaron were Dad's domain, but our mother gets the credit for running a revolving-door restaurant (as did so many families back in the 1950s) to accommodate the different dinner times dictated by our divergent Talmud Torah sessions.

All in all, it was Harold's passion for Jewish life, ignited in his youth, that motivated him to give so generously first of his time, and later, when business success allowed, his financial support. From his youth until today, Harold has maintained a strong commitment to Jewish education as the critical foundation for Jewish survival. When the so-called "Jewish counter-culture" emerged in the late 1960s, Harold Smith of St. Paul was supporting largely East Coast ventures like Response Magazine. A stalwart of support for the St. Paul Talmud Torah, Harold (with Mickey) gave funds to help create the Marjorie Smith Hofman Educational Building on Ford Parkway and Hamline to house the St. Paul Talmud Torah and the Day School. After our parents moved to Minneapolis when Oak Ridge Country Club became a hub for golf and social activities, Harold took an active interest in the Minneapolis Jewish Day School

Our parents' trip to Israel in 1962 marked the first of many foreign trips, some of them with longtime friends like Lester and Joanne Strouse or Paul and Clara Gorin, and others during which they formed new friendships with other Jewish couples from around the States.

It was during these trips that Harold first started collecting objects of Jewish interest. Soon he began combing Jewish stores, bazaars and flea markets in whatever country they would find themselves for Jewish treasures, and always made a point to visit synagogues and other places of Jewish interest in those countries. On one cruise in the Mediterranean, word spread onboard that Harold Smith was the *maven* who knew the local Jewish sites to visit. In one port of call, Harold and Mickey spent the day onshore with the well-known journalist Bernard Kalb, who was on the cruise as a guest lecturer, and his wife. At one point as they were out and about, Mickey turned around and saw a large number of other passengers trailing behind them, certain that wherever Harold was headed would be worth visiting!!!

From their travels and from visits to Judaica dealers in Mid-town and the Lower East Side while in New York City for the annual shoe show, Harold accumulated a significant collection of *groggers, hanukkiyot,* spice boxes, *megillot* and other ritual objects. He would never tire of showing his collection, much of which was housed in our basement on Colvin Avenue, to anyone and everyone who happened to visit, and even some who came specifically to see the collection. Many items were fashioned of silver and needed to be polished with some regularity. This, of course, fell to Mickey, and when she finally tired of this assignment (though to be honest much of the work went to long-time house cleaner Emily Novy, who had been with our mother's family since Mickey was a young girl), she told our father that it was time to find a new home for his collection, and some time thereafter the Harold and Mickey Smith Judaic Gallery came into being at the Minneapolis Institute of Arts.

The Al and Daisy Mains Infirmary (named for Mickey's parents and funded jointly with Mickey's brother Donald and his wife Rhoda) was among the first of many gifts to Herzl camp. When Holly Guncheon was appointed Director of Development at Herzl Camp, a steadfast friendship with Harold and Mickey was formed. Harold and Mickey saw to the creation of a new dining facility, the Harold and Mickey Smith *Chadar Ochel*, where much of the magic at Herzl Camp takes place. A gift to help replace campers' cabins dating from the 1940s led to the establishment of a group of cabins designated as *Kfar Smith*, Smith Village. Because so many families from the Twin Cities and other midwestern cities from which Herzl draws its camper population could not send their children to camp without some kind of financial assistance, Harold had originally established a scholarship fund in honor of his father, William B. Smith, known affectionately as W.B. After Mickey's death in 2010, our dad created the Mickey Smith Scholarship Fund, now known as the Mickey and Harold Smith Scholarship Fund. But the thing that gives our dad the most *naches* is having the road from the highway to camp named for Mickey, and he is always delighted when his friends tell him about letters from grandchildren whose return address is 7260 Mickey Smith Parkway. He is equally thrilled to see the latest generation of our family – great-great nieces Lucy and June Schwartz - attending Herzl and seeing them take to it so enthusiastically.

Harold and Mickey have been gratified to see grandchildren David and Eve continue the family's Jewish commitments, and Harold was particularly privileged to attend the Bat Mitzvah service of great-granddaughter Yael in suburban Chicago in the fall of 2017, where she led much of the service, including the Torah reading. When he has been able to visit David and his family for Friday night dinners, having great-grandson Ari lead the recitation of the *Birkat HaMazon* (Grace after Meals) beginning in his pre-school days has been another source of great *naches,* and an affirmation that the deep commitment which Harold's parents and grandparents passed down to him remains vibrant among their – and his – heirs 100 years later!

We think that after reading the essays in this volume, you will agree that in his own way, Harold Smith is a man whose name is not out of place alongside those luminaries mentioned at the outset.

We dedicate this book to our dad with love.

James C. Smith, M.D   Rabbi Mitchell Smith, Ph. D.

100 Years, 10,000 Blessings, and Still Counting

A Tribute to Harold Smith

Rabbi Hayim Herring

THANK YOU, HAROLD. In ways of which you're unaware, you have helped my family and me become the kind of people who love and value Jewish community, Israel, and understand how valuable art can be as a bridge to forging relationships across faith communities, generations, gender, and ethnicities. I'm going to use a few examples from my own life to illustrate the likely thousands of others whose lives you have touched during this past century. That, of course, means book-ending my thoughts with a little Torah, something that has informed and framed your own life.

According to the Talmud (*Menachot* 43b), a person is supposed to recite 100 blessings each day. The Biblical proof text for this teaching is a bit of a stretch. It's based on Deuteronomy 10:12, in which Moses asks the Israelites what they think God requires of them, to which he then supplies the answer. "And now, O Israel, what does the Lord your God demand of you? Only this: to revere the Lord your God, to walk only in God's paths, to love God, and to serve the Lord your God with all your heart and soul."

וְעַתָּה֙ יִשְׂרָאֵ֔ל מָ֚ה יְהֹוָ֣ה אֱלֹהֶ֔יךָ שֹׁאֵ֖ל מֵעִמָּ֑ךְ כִּ֣י אִם־לְ֠יִרְאָ֠ה אֶת־יְהֹוָ֨ה אֱלֹהֶ֜יךָ לָלֶ֣כֶת בְּכָל־דְּרָכָיו֮ וּלְאַהֲבָ֣ה אֹת֒וֹ וְלַֽעֲבֹד֙ אֶת־יְהֹוָ֣ה אֱלֹהֶ֔יךָ בְּכָל־לְבָבְךָ֖ וּבְכָל־נַפְשֶֽׁךָ׃

Many of the Talmud's rabbis were punsters and careful listeners to the Hebrew Biblical text. In Hebrew, the word for "what" (*mah*) sounds like "one hundred" (*me'ah*). And in playing with the similarity in sound between *mah* and *me'ah*, I believe they were suggesting that to love God requires actualizing that inner feeling of love through external actions because a blessing is always a prelude to some deed. You've always had a head for numbers, and we know that bar mitzvah is the age at which a young adolescent male becomes obligated for the performance of *mitzvot*. So going on the assumption that beginning at age thirteen you became obligated to recite 100 blessings per day, which required performing 100 Jewish actions per day, that would mean that by now you have had the opportunity to be a blessing 3,175,500 times (that is, reciting and performing 100 action blessings 365 days per year, beginning 87 years ago, when you were 13 years old). Perhaps that number is slightly exaggerated, but I do believe that you have directly and indirectly changed the lives of thousands for the better. And a brief part of my family history can illustrate how it is possible to reach so many people without even being fully aware of it.

My mother-in-law was born and raised in Lincoln, Nebraska and spent a few summers at Herzl Camp. For a young girl from Nebraska, that meant having the ability to live in a more immersive Jewish environment for at least several weeks a year. Skipping forward to the next generation, based on the positive experiences of my mother-in-law, my in-laws sent my wife-to-be, Terri, to Herzl Camp, and there was no question that our children would be Herzl campers when they were old enough. Had I been born and raised in the Twin Cities, it's safe to say that I also would have been a Herzl alum, but I at least had vicarious Herzl experiences through my children and through visits with the many hundreds of campers from Beth El Synagogue, where I served as a rabbi for ten years.

When I moved from New York City to Minneapolis in 1985 with my wife, Terri, we didn't yet have children. However, from our earliest days in Minneapolis, we were lobbied heavily to make sure that our then non-existing children would attend a Jewish day school in Minneapolis and not St. Paul. When we became parents and had to decide where to enroll them, we realized that for our family at that time, there was only one option: the Day School at the Talmud Torah of St. Paul. (And I can tell you that we received a lot of flak for that choice, but politics would not prevent us from being responsible parents and doing what we believed was best for our children.) I remember when we first took them to school and entered the building, we saw a painting of Marjorie Smith Hoffman, of blessed memory, with a brief explanation of a life that was cut short by cancer. I later came to better appreciate how fitting an expression of values it was for you and your family to memorialize her through Jewish education, a cause that so essentially defined you and your family.

So is it any exaggeration to state that you have influenced thousands of people, many of whom you don't even know? While I'm just one person, even before I had met you and your family, you already had an impact on my family, starting with my mother-in-law, continuing with Terri, and then extending to our own children when they were older. I'm sure that there is an algorithm that could be written today to better estimate how many blessings you have provided for others. But if my story is a reliable indication, your influence of thousands could be an undercount.

Fortunately, despite the Mississippi River which still remains an emotional barrier for many who live in both St. Paul and Minneapolis, I did have an opportunity to get to know and work with you and your family. Although you were a stalwart at Beth Jacob I would see you and Mickey, of blessed memory, with some regularity at Friday night services at Beth El Synagogue. But it wasn't until I worked at the Minneapolis Jewish Federation on issues of Jewish identity and continuity that I came to appreciate your insights into thinking big about the power of Jewish education and the many forms that it could take. It was refreshing to work with you on dreaming fearlessly about how collaboration around Jewish education could amplify our resources and shape more Jewish lives. As an outsider, I couldn't comprehend the institutional inertia and fear that bred a mutual wariness of our respective institutional leaders in St. Paul and Minneapolis, and their presumption that there must be some "hidden motives" around collaboration. (I understand the fear now and still think that it's inexcusable.) But for a local like you, and from St. Paul no less, to challenge "the conventional wisdom" against more collaboration was remarkable. While trying to do the right thing and not the popular thing has been a driving force for you, I can only imagine that the personal costs of taking positions on issues that were so clear to you, but that others couldn't see, didn't want to acknowledge, or simply couldn't understand was sometimes difficult.

During that time when we worked closely together, you, a handful of lay leaders, and some dedicated staff accomplished several innovations including upgrading the quality of Jewish education in our Twin Cities by deepening professional growth opportunities for Jewish educators and creating a most remarkable exhibition space, The Harold and Mickey Smith Gallery of Jewish Arts and Culture. Until then, the North Carolina Museum of Art in Raleigh was the sole public museum with a permanent Judaica collection.

Prior to moving to Minnesota, I was unaware of its ugly history of anti-Semitism, especially in Minneapolis. I first encountered its lingering effects when I was at the Federation and we wanted to advertise in the general press some educational programs targeting families with young children and interfaith families. At that time, there were many Federation lay leaders who still privately bore the scars of anti-Semitism and were appalled at the idea that we might advertise Jewish programs in general publications. They literally feared that we might "attract" people who were intent on doing us harm – and that was back in the mid-1990s. There was a *"sha-shtill"* mentality. Don't be too publicly Jewish. By creating an exhibition space at one of the premier public cultural institutions in our community, you made a different statement about pride in being Jewish, and confidence that a religious tradition that had contributed so much to the world should be opened to the broadest community possible. In fact, you believed correctly that opening ourselves up to the world in such a public, visible space, both Jews who would never step foot into a Jewish institution, and non-Jews who were curious about Judaism, might replace past negative perceptions about Judaism with positive views through programming. That is all the more reason that in times like today, your family's decision has taken on more significance than we could have imagined.

Perhaps you heard the story from Dr. Evan Maurer, who was then C.E.O. of the Minneapolis Institute of Art, who even after the plans for the expansion of the museum were finalized, still had one remaining permanent gallery for which he could not seem to find the right focus that would complete his vision for the renovated Institute. One day, he called me very excited and said something like, "Hayim, I know how we're going to use this one remaining gallery. It's going to be a space for a permanent Judaic collection at the Institute so that even when I'm no longer here, that space will remain." He felt that it was *bashert* that he struggled so late in the process to determine how to use that gallery, and that the answer to what it should be would emerge. And when it did, it was almost like an epiphany that Judaica belonged in a public museum and that your family would understand its significance.

Your generous contributions over the years to Hadassah Hospital in Jerusalem once again showed how love, thought, and strategy are a powerful combination for providing help to people in need. Hadassah Hospital has been a mainstay provider of healthcare not only for Jewish and Arab Israelis, but for people throughout the region, regardless of ethnicity, gender, and religion. In fact, it's one of those places where you can find the full mix of Israeli society in any waiting room at the hospital, both on staff and as patients. Hadassah remains a world-class leader in research because of people like you who care enough about Israel and its disproportionately large number of researchers who make worldwide contributions to people's health.

As I've completed these reflections on your 100th birthday about a week before Passover, I can't resist the temptation of thinking of the Seder table as the classroom par excellence. While a Seder is observed only once or twice during the year depending on one's practice and location (Israelis only have one Seder), its impact on our personal and collective memory has been great. A Seder both informs and transforms. It is a vehicle for transmitting tradition across the generations and an experience that has the potential to shape our commitment to making the world a more just, compassionate and empathetic place, in which respectful debate and discussion are encouraged by young and old. We retell our history to refresh our memory.

And why is that so important? I recently heard a colleague, Rabbi Mike Feuer, say that, "Memory in its full sense is a process of telling a story of the past, that builds an identity in the present, which is oriented toward the future of which we dream." *The Jewish community of your childhood, 100 years ago, is vastly different than today's Jewish community, but you've taken those memories from the past to provide thousands with a Jewish identity today and have helped to give them the resources to launch tomorrow's Jewish dreams.*

May God continue to bless you with health and strength of mind and body, family members who love and care for you very much in ways that reflect our highest Jewish values, and good friends. And Harold, I also want to add a personal prayer that you'll continue to have *emunah*, which I define not as "faith," but as trust in the future even when you can't intuit or try to manage the outcome that you think is best, but you still trust that things will work out even if it isn't clear how they will play out.

After all, who would have guessed that you already had an impact on a kid from Philly – I was only 27 years old when I moved to Minneapolis – because my mother-in-law attended Herzl Camp, decided to send her daughter to Herzl Camp, whose appetite for a more immersive Jewish community not just during summers but throughout the year, would lead her to The Jewish Theological Seminary and Columbia University in New York where we met as undergraduates. I didn't know about you and I couldn't even locate Minnesota on a map. But I have *emunah*, trust in the future, because while my story is, well, my story, you've invested wisely in efforts that have touched thousands throughout your life, and those thoughtful efforts will continue to prepare tomorrow's leaders today.

With appreciation and affection,

Hayim

Rabbi Hayim Herring, Ph.D., has served as rabbi at Beth El Synagogue, Minneapolis, Assistant Executive Director at the Minneapolis Jewish Federation, and executive director at STAR (Synagogues: Transformation and Renewal), a national Jewish foundation. Hayim's publications include Leading Congregations and Nonprofit Organizations in a Connected World: Platforms, People and Purpose, co-authored with Dr. Terri Elton.

What's in a Blessing?

Rabbi Leigh Lerner

When I think of Harold, I cannot help but think of countless Torah lunches at the St. Paul Athletic Club where for many years Mt. Zion members and others let words of Torah from every generation influence our thinking about the day's problems, and hopefully also let our responses shape the Torah tradition we would hand to the next generation. There a warm and durable camaraderie developed as we immersed ourselves in Jewish law, legend, and philosophy. I thank Harold for his part in those memories and I thank him, as well, for his friendship across the years and the many miles between us.

I cannot think of Harold without also thinking of Mickey, aleha hashalom, *and their goodly and giving life together that has done so much for our Twin City Jewish community and for the larger Jewish world. I also remember them both for their strong role as parents to a fine and growing family. Both Harold and the late Mickey have been a true blessing to those around them. Perhaps that is why I chose the subject of blessing as my contribution to this Festschrift in Harold's honor. I know Harold's life will continue as a blessing to all around him.*

THE WORDS OF Jacob's so-called blessing of his children at the end of his life and at the end of Genesis are not entirely a blessing. Some phrases read like a curse. Some read like a statement of fact. Some read like an angry father's last chance to take a whack at his obstreperous young ones who are now immature adults. And yes, some few words read like a kind and generous blessing. What can we learn from this conglomeration of emotion, history, and prediction (or was it really hindsight as many scholars propose)?

First, we learn that blessings are mixed. Like the proverbial Golem who always takes the words of his master literally and goes too far, every blessing in abundance can become a blessing in overdose. Look at Jacob's blessing of his son Issachar. Jacob says that Issachar is a strong ass crouching between two burdens; and he saw that resting was good, and that the land was pleasant; and bowed his shoulder to bear and became a servant to tribute. (Gen. 49:14 ff)

What was Issachar's blessing? First, he was "strong-like-a-bull." The text says ass, but that describes an animal like a donkey, a beast of burden, and we would choose a different animal to describe strength today. The Torah means that Issachar was strong. He knew how to work hard, to carry a burden, and he appreciated halting his wanderings in the Land of Israel upon his share of land near Mt. Tabor just south of the Galilee, with lovely farm acreage sweeping down toward the Jordan. Issachar was happy, counted his blessings, enjoyed the wealth of the land and the work of his hands, but Biblical historians tell us that in order to keep it all, for many years the tribe had to pay tribute taxes to the Canaanites. The blessing of good land was a mixed blessing because it led to the curse of tribute, until at last the Canaanites were defeated in the Land of Israel.

So it is with nearly every blessing. It makes its requirements upon us. How wonderful to have a home of your own. But the day you sign the deed is the day you pay your first real estate tax, reimbursing the owner for the prepaid portion of taxes falling to you in the coming months of the year, and here in Quebec there is the dreaded Welcome Tax, a levy based on the purchase price. There will be other responsibilities of home ownership, as well, many unforeseeable and seldom considered a blessing.

To receive blessing in abundance can also lead us astray. Wealth is wonderful, but when the accumulation of wealth becomes central, what happens to family, love, friendship, the joy of achievement in the next generation, and more? Every blessing when taken too far can become a mixed blessing. It's a blessing to have children when they're fervently desired. Twins might be double the blessing. Triplets, maybe triple the blessing. Quintuplets, hmmm . . . a blessing for each of the children to have life, but maybe more blessing than mom and dad can handle in this costly and demanding world of ours? So the first thing we're taught by Jacob's blessing is, virtually every blessing is a mixed blessing.

Next we learn that a blessing can become a curse, and a curse can become a blessing. Jacob says: "Simeon and Levi are brothers; instruments of cruelty are their swords. O my soul, do not come into their council; to their assembly, let my honor not be united; for in their anger they slew a man, and in their wanton will they lamed an ox. Cursed be their anger, for it was fierce; and their wrath, for it was cruel; I will divide them in Jacob, and scatter them in Israel." (Gen. 49:5 ff)

Jacob remembers how Simeon and Levi wreaked revenge upon Hamor and all his tribe for having raped their sister Dinah. Jacob thought his boys' vengeance upset his relations with the locals, so he cursed their brutal anger. How were they divided and scattered in Israel? Levi became the priestly tribe, with no major land holding at all, while Simeon settled way in the south, south of Judah, around Beer sheva, cut off from the rest of the tribes. So the blessing of Jacob is really a curse upon these two.

On the other hand, can a curse be a blessing? Why not? Levi became the priests, serving God and teaching Torah. Simeon probably disappeared into Judah at the time of the Babylonian exile, and thus became a tribe that survived as Jews, even though we usually count it among the 10 lost tribes. A curse can become a blessing, depending on what we make of it and also upon what others ineluctably do to us – the uncontrollable *mazal* factor.

In our own lifetime, have we not seen blessings become curses and curses become blessings? The blessing of Israel's victories in war allowed it to survive and prosper, but those same victories have also cursed it with some thorny national issues and international relations. Without those blessings of victory, Israel would not be alive today to deal with the curse of anti-Zionism and anti-Semitism which certain nations and groups display. Likewise, the blessing of Jewish success in North America led to curses like Madoff and others, men who prey on their own people, creating disastrous results for Jewish life and its lifeline of support. I imagine that each of us can name times in our own lives when blessings dearly desired led to problems unexpected, or inversely, the trouble necessary to surmount a blessing gone awry led to new wisdom, abilities, or success. So life goes.

Third, Jacob teaches that what looks like a blessing may actually be a curse. Of Judah he says, "The scepter shall not depart from Judah … until Shiloh comes, and to him will be a gathering of peoples." (Gen. 49:10 ff) Judah is the tribe destined to rule, Judah, the very tribe of David. A fine blessing this is for Judah, but what of Shiloh? It's a curse that people read as a blessing. Rashi and many others think that Shiloh means *Mashiach*, the Messiah. There would be no need for a *mashiach* if the rule of Judah were to be forever, but obviously it was not to be so. The monarchy has to fall so that someday a descendant of David would return to claim the throne. Until then, the Israelites were scattered and oppressed. What looks like a blessing is really a curse, or at the very least, the promise that the Jewish people will be severely challenged to develop as a different kind of entity than a monarchical, theological state centered on its own land and its Temple.

Furthermore, the Christians exacerbated the situation, for they have often claimed this line to be a direct reference to Jesus. Now what appears on the surface to be a blessing to Jews has become a Christian messianic promise which, over the centuries, was often a curse to Jewish life; witness such events as the Talmud trials and disputations, and our expulsions from virtually every European nation.

The verse in the Torah referring to Shiloh is not a matter of a blessing becoming a curse, or a curse becoming a blessing. It's a matter of a curse being concealed as a blessing. Judah will rule, then fail, and Israel will be without leadership and land, at the mercy of its enemies. That's a curse carefully concealed. If the Torah could rewrite history, what would have been the blessing?

The ancient Israelites never expected to have a king. They were told to settle the land without one. Against God's wishes, they ultimately demanded a king like other nations had. The so-called blessing of Judah's power is a curse which says, you'll be in big trouble if you ever get yourselves a king. Live happily as independent tribes and make God your king. That's what it really meant.

So we are reminded, when we make something king over us, we are often destined to lose it all. If I only had this, if I only became that, if I only could reach this personal goal, then all would be well. Often we get there, only to find that we have subjugated ourselves to nothingness or to some other unacceptable power over us. As it has been true for individuals, so it has sometimes been true for Jewish communities which backed the wrong side in the politics of their era. Many Jews in Italy, for example, were stunned by the Racial Laws of 1938 because 16 years earlier their support was welcomed by Mussolini and his Fascists, who accepted prominent Jews as members of the Fascist Party.

The blessing of Judah reminds us, probably with 20/20 hindsight on the part of the biblical author, that today and every day ought to be the time when we set over ourselves neither a king nor a single unchangeable governing principle, but only the Eternal One of Israel, who honors our diverse humanity because we are made in God's image, but who is so unknowable that anything else we make into a god is merely an idol. That is the teaching of our mysterious, mystical, rational, classical Jewish thought, and it speaks loudly about the nature of the blessings we desire.

From Jacob's blessing we learn: every blessing is a mixed blessing. Blessings can become curses and curses can become blessings. Often what we believe to be a blessing is, in fact, a hidden curse. Just as often, what seems to be a curse challenges us to remake it into a blessing. It is one thing to bless God, or even to give a blessing to another human being, but Jacob's blessings to his children calls us to be careful about the blessings we want and accept for ourselves.

Rabbi Leigh Lerner, Rabbi Emeritus at Temple Emanu-El-Beth Sholom in Montreal, Canada, served as Rabbi of Mount Zion Temple, St. Paul, MN from 1972-1989. He has also served as visiting Rabbi at Shir Hadash Congregation in Florence, Italy.

The Breadth and Breath of Torah

Rabbi Alexander Davis

THE OTHER DAY I was returning home, driving past Cedar Lake and I saw one of those picture-perfect scenes. A thin layer of mist gently hovered above the still water. And near the water's edge, where the mist was thinner, you could make out the reflection of the fall-colored trees in the glassy water. I kept one eye on the road and soaked in the beauty of the scene with the other. And with my third eye, I saw echoes of this morning's Torah reading: "*V'ruah Elohim m'rahefet al pnai hamayim,* God's wind sweeping over the face of the water. And God looked out and declared creation good." (Genesis 1:2) In that momentary glimpse, I sensed the unity of earth and heaven, plant and animal, God and man.

V'ruah Elohim m'rahefet al pnai hamayim. This verse came to mind not only driving home but earlier in the week. On Sunday night I spoke on an interfaith panel with a Catholic educator and a Muslim Imam about water, *mayim.* This is the Torah's first mention of water and so in a sense, this verse unites the three Abrahamic peoples because out of water, out of this cosmic ocean God brought the world into being.

This morning I am brought back once again to God's wind sweeping over the face of the water. For this morning, when we gather to celebrate the dedication of our *Hevre Yad Hazaka,* our Torah reading society, I discover a message about how to read Torah and where to find God.

The rabbis teach that the Torah is like water. Like water, Torah is life-giving. We can hardly go a day without her. That's why the midrash says we have to read Torah not just on Shabbat but on Monday and Thursday morning to quench our spiritual thirst. So let's read our verse again.

"*V'ruah Elohim m'rahefet al pnai hamayim.* The spirit/breath of God hovers above the surface of the waters" of Torah. God hovers just above the words. God's breath floats just above the Hebrew letters. Commentating on this verse, the Maggid of Mezrich taught that rebbes are like birds. Birds swoop down and briefly touch the waters then fly up. So too, rebbes briefly touch the waters of Torah then soar up. And in that instant, they receive *Ruah Elohim*, divine inspiration that elevates their teaching to a holy level.

While only rebbes may have access to divine inspiration, all of us men and women have the opportunity to breathe in *Ruah Elohim*, God's breath that hovers above the waters of Torah. We breathe it in when we read Torah, or study Torah, or follow along during a Torah reading. We have the opportunity, but we must ask ourselves if that is what happens.

In his beautiful essay on the spirituality of Torah in the back of the *Eitz Hayim Humash*, Professor Michael Fishbane bemoans the way we read Torah. We tend to read Torah like we read a novel or read the paper or an email. We skim it. "Ah, I know that story," we tell ourselves. I once saw someone studying the synagogue handout in greater detail than the Torah reading. "What's so interesting," I asked. "I know the story," he replied, "but did you see *this?*" Torah reading is not about rereading a story we all know. It is not about repeating a tale we've heard a hundred times. *Ruah Elohim m'rahefet al pnai hamayim.* The very breath of God hovers above those words.

Fishbane writes, "The rhythm of reading must be restored to the rhythm of breathing, to the cadence of the cantillation marks of the sacred text. Only then will the individual absorb the text with his or her life breath. Only then will the sacred text be restored as a living teaching and instruction for the constant renewal of the self."

The rhythm of reading must be restored to the rhythm of breathing. When we read Torah, we tell a story. But it is more than that. It is a chance to breathe in deeply, to breathe in the *Ruah Elohim*, God's breath that hovers above the face of the waters of Torah. When we slow down our reading, when our breathing becomes the cadence of the trope, then the mist above the letters clears and we see our lives reflected in the waters of the Torah. And when we breathe in God's breath, then

God's *Ruah*, fills our lungs and our souls. And with that breath, we sense we are created anew. We recognize the potential within for life to spring forth.

Rabbi Alexander Davis is Senior Rabbi at Temple Beth El in Minneapolis, MN

Torah Orah, Torah is Light

Rabbi David Steinhardt

The following is from a sermon delivered on Shabbat Hanukkah, December 17, 2017

I WANT TO bring us close. We have struggled a lot in the recent past. Too often disagreements separate us. The world is dangerous. And we know that. But there is so much to bring us together.

Here in this sanctuary, on Shabbat Hanukkah, let us be embraced by the light that can be found here.

What is that light? It has many dimensions. In the Zohar, the fountain of mystical teaching, we learn: Torah Orah, Torah is light.

Torah is learning . . . and learning can bring understanding.

Torah is language . . . and language can communicate to increase peace in the world.

Torah is a story. It is our story. And it's the story we carry of our past; what was. The stories contain meaning for us to unpackage. Torah is insight. But it's also the story of the future. We have a story of aspiration of how people *can* be — perhaps we say *should* be — and that is the light of Torah.

The rabbis increase the light through their literary creations in what is known as Midrash. There is one such Midrash on the beginning of creation. The mystics saw the world as being immersed in light. There was a light on the outside and it reflected an inner light. And then Adam sinned. He broke the only law he had, and he lied.

The sun set, and he feared there would never be light again. And so, he lit the first light. And we see that even in an imperfect world we can bring light.

Adam realized that as the nights got longer and longer, he had the agency to create light himself; or to learn from the Creator about light. In a few days it will be the longest night of the year. And we will create a light to dispel some of that darkness. We can do that.

We use a lot of candle light in our tradition. Every Shabbat and *Yom Tov* we light a light. What does it mean when we say *"Asher kidshanu b'mitzvotav, v'tzivanu l'hadlik ner shel Shabbat* or *Yom Tov* or *Hanukkah?"* Maybe it is commanding us, not only to rely on a spiritual light, or the light of nature, but we should be the one who lights. We are agents of light. We bring the light on God's holy days.

We look for inspiration from outside, and that is a reflection of the *brachah* we say at the end of Shabbat at Havdalah: *Baruch Ata Adonoi Ehloheinu melech ha'olam, borei me'orei ha'eish.* There God creates the light. There, when we're beginning *hol* — the normal week, the time we work and do stuff — there is a God we look to. And what a beautiful balance! We create. On this day, we learn a lot about light . . . more than we ever thought.

Hassidic master Reb Shneur Zalman of Liadi, once said, "A little light dispels a lot of darkness." When we're feeling a little down, a little kindness, a little love, a word of encouragement can change the complexion of the moment.

One candle in a dark room brings light to everything.

There's a reason that humankind's story begins with the creation of light: *Vayomer Adonai "Yehi Or."* And we know that light is not just what is seen by the eyes but also experienced in the heart as it expands the mind.

In the story of Hanukkah, light means a lot of different things. It's about freedom. It's about continuity and survival. And it's about courage and faith.

Today we read two *haftarah* selections. The first was read by the Bar Mitzvah boy Solomon, deferred from some weeks ago when Hurricane Irma forced us to close our doors. And then we read the *haftarah* for Shabbat Hanukkah.

And in the juxtaposition of these two *haftarot* we learn something about the images of light.

Torah Orah, Torah is Light

The *haftarah* that Solomon recited was taken from the Prophet Isaiah. It is a text of great hopefulness. It spoke to an exiled people – a people that had experienced destruction. And in it were words of comfort and warmth and hope. The prophet proclaims there will be a return to Zion and it will be spiritually transformative because the spirit of God will pervade. And Zion will evoke God's light and it will manifest itself because all the people of the world will look towards Israel and Zion, and they will find within her gates peace and prosperity. All people will see Zion as their home. God's light will be experienced by those returning from exile and this will cause a new day to arise!

And after Solomon recited his haftarah, our cantor recited the *haftarah* from Zechariah which was chosen by the rabbis for this special Shabbat. It's not about a military victory. It's not about domination of one people over another. It's about the menorah from the ancient temple and its light: the seven lamps symbolizing the eyes of God overlooking the entire world. And that light is meant to spark a spiritual renewal for our people and humanity. And that renewal comes with a promise and a hope. *"Lo b'chayil v'lo b'kho'ach."* Not by might and not by power, but by the spirit of God. That's the light of Hanukkah that we have preserved for thousands of years.

What is that spirit?

It's the spirit of learning.

Compassion.

Generosity.

Freedom.

It is the spirt that comes from the deepest places of our souls, and it affirms life.

Solomon's *haftarah* is one that gave hope to the future establishment of a people on its land and the projections of "what could be." It gave way ultimately to abuse of wealth and power. Once again there was a destruction and an exile.

But the second haftarah remains part of our vision for the future . . . "not by might nor by power." These are the words of the prophet Zechariah, words that challenge us to use our place to allow the deepest yearnings to shed light on the world.

You see that on this bimah today, this Hanukkah, we have a new *hanukkiah*. It's my gift to the congregation as a way of memorializing my parents. I decided to do so after the passing of my mother, Susan.

My mom and her family came from Germany. On Hanukkah we lit an old *hanukkiah* that was passed down through the generations. I only have recollection of one gift that I received for Hanukkah, but I remember the moments with my family, sitting around the menorah, singing songs and celebrating our Jewish lives.

For me that *hanukkiah* was about a family that left a place where Jews could no longer survive. But it represented a sense that some did survive, and that which was most important was carried through the generations. Lights continue to burn and the warmth of the family and the hope for the future remained a part of the very fabric of our lives. On Hanukkah we would hear many stories which pointed to that very moment of lighting and the idea that future generations would also kindle these lights.

And so I dedicate this *hanukkiah* in memory of all our parents . . . to us, to our good fortune, to life . . . to the future of B'nai Torah and the Jewish people. Every night this past week we gathered in our lobby with our students and whoever was here to light this *hanukkiah*, and I felt the presence of generations gone by. And I felt how happy they would have been and optimistic about our future and our children's future.

That is in the gift of light.

May the light of the *hanukkiah* bring us all warmth ... and hope ... and peace.

Rabbi David Steinhardt is Senior Rabbi, Congregation Bnai Torah in Boca Raton, FL

Lessons from the Exodus

Morley Goldberg

"The arc of the moral universe is long, but it bends toward justice."

SO SAID DR. MARTIN LUTHER KING, JR *z"l* in 1964 in the Baccalaureate sermon he delivered at the commencement exercises for Wesleyan University.

In 1940 a version of this same phrase was included in a New Year's message by Rabbi Jacob Kohn *z"l* of Sinai Temple in Los Angeles.

> *Our faith is kept alive by the knowledge, founded on long experience, that the arc of history is long and bends toward justice. We have seen so many ancient tyrannies pass from earth since Egypt and Rome held dominion that our eyes are directed not to the tragic present, but to the beyond, wherein the arc of history will be found bending toward justice, victory and freedom.*

Actually, neither Dr. King nor Rabbi Kohn is the originator of the quote. It attributed to Theodore Parker, a Unitarian minister and abolitionist, born in 1810 in Lexington, Massachusetts. The quote is found in a collection of sermons that was published in 1853.

I want to examine how this much quoted and hopeful statement holds up in 2018, and what the Exodus might teach us in this regard.

If there is truth to this statement, and evidence in human history to support it, then to me it may provide the best substantiation that God exists. This God, in partnership with humankind, is constantly influencing the moral universe toward greater freedom, justice and goodness in opposition to the countervailing forces of chaos and evil.

In his book *God of Becoming and Relationship*, Rabbi Bradley Artson provides a cogent theological framework to this model of God. Artson embraces Process Theology, developed by Alfred North Whitehead which presents the premise that God is in a dynamic relationship with each and every human being. "At this very moment – and at every moment – God meets each of us and all creation, offering us the best possible next step. We have the opportunity and freedom to decide whether to take that best possible next step or not."

In effect a gigantic series of choices of 'best possible next steps' made by enough of humankind over the course of history may be the positive force bending toward justice.

By way of contrast, in two of his books, *The Better Angels of Our Nature* (2011) and more recently *Enlightenment Now* (2018) Steven Pinker, a Professor in the Department of Psychology at Harvard University, provides considerable evidence that the arc of the moral universe is truly bending toward justice, but posits that this is not attributable to God's agency (Pinker is an atheist). While convincingly contending that there is less violence in the world, and that life has been getting progressively better for most people on most measurable counts, including health, wealth, inequality, the environment, peace, democracy, Pinker contends that this betterment of the human condition is attributable to continuously improving scientific rationality and liberal humanism, i.e., human agency alone.

Pinker asserts that there are five historical human forces that have led to the triumph of empathy, self-control, a moral sense, and the faculty of reason over the equally powerful human thirst to exploit and dominate other groups, and to take revenge against those who have offended us with no sense of self-control, temperance, or forgiveness. These are (1) "Leviathan" (following Hobbes), i.e., the rise of the state and judiciary that enforces a monopoly of coercion, and funnels disputes between individuals and groups through the judicial apparatus; (2) commerce, the globalization of which started in the sixteen century, and which changes international relations into a positive sum game that is crippled by war; (3) feminization, through which the interests and values of women are increasing respected and generalized to both sexes; (4) cosmopolitanism, including literacy, mobility, and mass media, which lead people increasingly to understand the mind-sets and desires of others unlike themselves, and to expand their circle of sympathy to larger and larger groupings of individuals; and (5) "escalator of reason," through which people can learn from the past the futility of acting out their primitive urges, and rather turn to peaceful solutions to their problems.

Yet for all its appeal there are several inconvenient truths haunting Pinker's thesis. These include the rise in income inequality, global warming and the continued high level of gun violence in the United States. But perhaps most damning of all is the latest annual Freedom House report – *Freedom in the World* – which reveals that for the tenth consecutive year in a row there are fewer nations and fewer people living freely. More totalitarian regimes are on the rise, freedom of the press is diminishing, there is less tolerance for immigrants, and the United States has relinquished its traditional moral leadership position in the world. These facts seemingly undermine several of Pinker's postulates above.

This is worrisome. In the great arc of history this setback in freedom may be but a momentary blip. But the fear is that it may be more enduring.

So what is a Jew to do? In this Passover holiday, in our annual celebration of the rebirth of nature and our season of freedom, what lessons might we learn from the Exodus story that will help us bend the arc back in the right direction?

Rabbi Jonathan Sacks offers the following:

> *To defend a country you need an army, but to defend a civilization you need education. That is why Moses, according to Rousseau, spoke about the duty of parents in every generation to educate their children about why freedom matters and how it was achieved.*
>
> *Freedom is not won by merely overthrowing a tyrannical ruler or an oppressive regime. That is usually only the prelude to a new tyranny, a new oppression. The faces change, but not the script. True freedom requires the rule of law and justice,*

and a judicial system in which the rights of some are not secured by the denial of rights to others.

Freedom begins with what we teach our children. That is why Jews became a people whose passion is education; whose heroes are teachers and whose citadels are schools. Nowhere is this more evident than on Passover, when the entire ritual of passing our story on to the next generation is set in motion by the questions asked by a child. In every generation we need to cultivate afresh the habits of the heart that Tocqueville called "the apprenticeship of liberty."

The message of Passover remains as powerful as ever. Freedom is won not on the battlefield but in the classroom and the home. Teach your children the history of freedom if you want them never to lose it."

Rabbi Bradley Artson notes:

Not only Jews, but countless Christians, Muslims, secularists and others have claimed their place as heirs to the heritage of ancient Israel: of one Ultimate Reality that is equally accessible to all, of a universal standard of human dignity without exception, of one legal standard of justice that applies to all, of the concept of Shabbat - days of rest and renewal, of the dignity of labor, the universal right for education and health, of living in harmony with the rhythms of the land. These are now the birthright of all human beings, and they emerge from the motley crew who left Pharaoh's Egypt to birth a Torah of love, justice, and inclusion.

Rabbi Donniel Hartman explains:

One of the central lessons of our tradition, a lesson that transcends denominational and political divides, is that Judaism is not exhausted by the desire to survive. The Exodus from Egypt was never about our physical liberation alone.

Lessons from the Exodus

"You have seen ... how I bore you on eagles' wings ... Now if you will obey Me ... you shall be to Me a kingdom of priests and a holy nation." (Exodus 19) **The Jewish people were not defined by the pursuit of freedom, but the pursuit of purpose.**

Professor Michael Walzer writes in Exodus and Revolution:

We still believe, or many of us do, what the Exodus first taught, or what it has commonly been taken to teach, about the meaning and possibility of politics and about its proper forms: first, that wherever you live, it is probably Egypt; second, that there is a better place, a world more attractive, a promised land; and third, that "the way to the land is through the wilderness." There is no way to get from here to there except by joining together and marching.

Education, inclusion, purpose, pursuit of justice. I think that most of us know what to do, but as Walzer points out, it's the doing that ultimately matters.

I am inspired by Harold Smith's persistent, purposeful and meaningful life's march through the wilderness. May his exemplary journey continue in good health for many years to come.

Morley Goldberg, a native of Winnipeg, currently resides in Toronto and spends his winters in Florida. He leads Torah study most Shabbatot at Congregation Bnai Torah of Boca Raton, where Harold is a regular participant.

Dor Holech v'Dor Ba: From Generation to Generation

Rabbi Morris Allen

I have been blessed with many wonderful people entering into my life as a result of serving as the rabbi of Beth Jacob Congregation. Among the many gems in that group has been Harold Smith, and on the occasion of his 100th birthday, I want to salute him for many reasons. First and foremost is his dedication to serious Jewish learning. His passion for Talmud Torah (both as an institution and as a moral imperative) is impressive. He cared deeply about what was transmitted to the generation which followed in his footsteps and the generations which will follow them. His love of learning is, in my opinion, one of the secrets of his longevity. He regularly regales me with stories of his youth and how his grandmother would demand that he share with her the pearls of wisdom he learned in cheder that week. In some way, I believe every time he engages in study he is connected not only to his people's past —but in a very real way to the old West Side of St Paul which defined his landscape as a youth. Harold also is a lover of Israel—in part as a result of Mickey's (z"l) devotion to Hadassah. Harold's devotion to Herzl Camp is profound and significant. The Twin Cities is a better place as a result of his dedication to these causes.

Harold also taught me about business and ethics. He taught me about the importance of serving rural communities and the benefits of doing so. He taught me about how to treat your workers and provide for them the opportunity to become managers and leaders. And he taught me about common decency and that the dignity of labor is something never to be dismissed. I have spent many mornings with Harold, having coffee and sharing in his joys and woes. Life has not always been easy for him and it continues to sometimes puzzle him. Marjorie's death continues to be evident in so many of the decisions that he makes moving forward. It was a loss from which he never fully recovered and yet her life remains a means for his ability to honor her and her values.

I delivered the words which follow as my Yizkor message to the congregation this past Yom Kippur. I thought about Harold and Mickey(z"l) as they moved beyond the unspeakable grief to continue to live lives of meaning. My prayer for Harold at this moment in his life is never stop growing, never stop learning, never stop giving and never give up on the values which have sustained you to this day. This is a Shehecheyanu moment and I am honored to have you in my life as a congregant, as a friend and as a fellow Jew trying to make meaning out of this enterprise called life. L'chayim!

YOM KIPPUR IS indeed a moment that frames our lives between life and death. If we take this day seriously, we understand what Riv Ellen Prell's teacher Victor Turner described as betwixt and between, describing the sense of this day as a classic liminal moment, whose rituals place us not fully in the land of the living – so we neither eat nor drink, we avoid physical intimacy, and we dress in white like angels as we imagine if only for a moment what this life has been and what the life to be might be – what we have accomplished here and what might be remembered after we are gone. Liminality refers to the limen – the threshold of a doorway – and has become a means for identifying moments and spaces of transition.

We often find ourselves in such liminal spaces and are usually uncomfortable in these spaces, and yet they can be the greatest gifts we are ever given. They can be the spaces and times when we grow the most. When we find ourselves occupying a position at, or on both sides of a boundary or threshold we are living in liminal space—between two things, between two stages in life, between loving and losing a love, between losing employment and gaining a new job, between receiving an education and finding a calling, between child rearing and letting go.

When we leave the tried and true but have not yet been able to replace it with anything else—we are living in liminal space. It is when we are between our old comfort zone and any possible new answer. If we do not learn how to hold anxiety, how to live with ambiguity, how to entrust and wait, we will run ... and do almost anything to flee this terrible cloud of unknowing.

At the end of the life cycle there is no greater liminal space than when we are facing death and loss. For the person who is aware that their life is ebbing away – as they experience and acknowledge that they are not capable of living fully as they once were and yet have not left this world of the living – these moments can be among the most precious; As our loved one leaves this world we are also beginning our own entrance into that liminal space. When a parent or a partner or God forbid a child dies, we are left neither here nor there. We are now separated from the past and not yet fully aware of how to live in the future. We are in liminal space. And indeed every ritual undertaken from the moment of a death and continuing through the funeral and the comfort provided for the mourner is to help us move beyond that liminal stage in order to fully re-enter back into the community of the living. With no plan and with no ritual, however, life becomes disorienting and agitating.

However, in our grief and our anger and our disbelief, we try to rush through this liminal stage in which we are living. Nothing good or creative emerges from trying to make it business as usual. Quick fixes to this liminal time of life are counter-productive. Mourning doesn't stop simply because we sit *Shiva* for one day instead of seven. Grief doesn't disappear because we don't recite *Kaddish* for a year and simply return to living as if there was no death.

The function of Judaism is to lead us at times into similar liminal spaces pregnant with possibility. Instead, all too often we have turned Judaism into a confirmation of the status quo and business as usual and simply a slow march towards death. Poor religious teaching teaches us how to live contentedly in a sick world, just as poor therapy teaches us how to accommodate ourselves to a sometimes-small world based on someone else's power, prestige, and possessions. A rabbi should always be opening up larger vistas for his or her community, vistas which are by definition risky. We have to allow ourselves to be drawn out of "business as usual" and remain patiently on the "threshold" where we are betwixt and between the familiar and the completely unknown. There alone is our old world left behind and we are not yet sure of our new existence. But in truth, that is a good space, where genuine possibilities can begin anew. It's the realm where renewal can take place because our false convictions have been revealed, as we reexamine who we are and how we are to be. This is the sacred space where the past can be buried with dignity and a larger and a newer world is born and revealed. *Dor holech v'dor ba* - a generation leaves, and a new generation enters, and the "v" (*vav*) in *v'dor* is that liminal space that is God's waiting room or perhaps we should say God's delivery room.

Change is never easy, but it is necessary at times. Here I am speaking about my decision to step down as your rabbi. Thirty-three years ago, several people were willing to suggest that what they had and where they wanted to be as Jews was not working in their religious lives. What they said to one another was that we must leave what we knew well and enter into a place where the future was uncharted and that the answers were unknown. I am not sure why the listing for Beth Jacob Congregation in Mendota Heights caught my eye 32 years ago this fall. Perhaps it was the stunning letter that Larry Savett wrote describing the shul—perhaps it was the realization that Phyllis and I were going to become parents in the course of that year and that maybe New York wasn't our kind of town. Maybe it was simply *bashert* that the god of rabbinic placement and the god of the Midwest conspired to bring us back here. Whatever it was—neither the shul nor I understood at that moment what we could build together as a team. You took a risk and lived with the unknown and I took a risk and lived with the unknown and together we emerged from our shared liminal spaces to create what is truly a model of Jewish communal life –particularly on Shabbat morning at shul.

This shul is capable of continuing this amazing story because the major component of the story remains unchanged and will grow—and that is your own presence here. What has made this shul a wonder to serve for 31 plus years has been the people who filled it on a regular basis, the people who are willing to sacrifice for it, the people who work in all of the different ways inside the shul and for the shul.

Over the years, I have tried to uphold the dignity and integrity of the rabbinate and the meaning of the title rabbi. I have been blessed with a congregation that has worked hard to maintain its understanding of itself as a *kehilla kedosha*—a sacred community. And as we move forward from this moment, I am reminded of one of my favorite quotes by E.L. Doctorow, who said about this kind of situation, "It's like driving a car at night. You never see further than your headlights, but you can make the whole trip across the country that way." Being in this liminal space is like driving the car in the dark, and the headlights are the illumination bringing hope and possibility. I pray we drive the entire year safely with the lights on and with hope and possibility leading the way.

I could not ever have imagined that on October 13, 1986 delivering my first *Yizkor* sermon to this shul that this would be the sermon I would deliver today before *Yizkor*. What I do know is that in all of the years in-between and in the years that will follow this talk this morning—with new lives born and other lives lost, *Yizkor* is that moment when we truly enter into the liminal nature of the day fully and with *kavanah*. How grateful I am for the opportunity to have done so this *yontif* morning once again. And what I pledge to you today is also what each of us will feel or utter to the beloved ones we hold dear in our hearts as we rise and recite *Yizkor* on their behalf: My bond with you will always be unbreakable, my love for you will always be unimpeachable; my gratitude for all we shared will always fill me with wonder.

Rabbi Morris Allen is Rabbi Emeritus of Beth Jacob Congregation in Mendota Heights, MN.

The Smith Scholar in Residence Program at Beth Jacob

Lisa Tiegel

Dear Harold,

One hundred!

The number itself has a ring of significance, it is a marker of history, a notation of change seen, understood and shared. You, Harold, have embraced all of it with a dedication to learning, an insistence on thoughtful contemplation, a prompting of substantive conversation. It is to that dedication, insistence and prompting that I want to speak now.

We met about a decade ago, when I was asked to help administer the Smith Scholar in Residence Program funded by you and Mickey. My role was small; all I did was help set up a structure so that the selection of dates and scholars would run smoothly from year to year. The real substance of the program, the learning from scholars, came about for four reasons: first, because you, Harold, have a life-long interest in study and learning; second, because you and Mickey decided to share that interest and joy by generously funding a scholar program at Beth Jacob; third, because a congregant at Beth Jacob, Professor Emerita Riv-Ellen Prell, offered her time and deep knowledge to help create and run the annual Smith Scholar in Residence Program; and fourth, because Rabbi Morris Allen worked closely with you and other lay leaders to bring outstanding scholars to Beth Jacob and to create a warm and welcoming environment at the shul and in his and Phyllis's home.

From 2002 to 2017, the Smith Scholar in Residence Program brought to Beth Jacob fifteen men and women engaged in the field of Jewish Studies. These great Judaic scholars teach at (among other places) the Jewish Theological Seminary, Boston Hebrew College, Brandeis, Harvard, the University of Virginia, the University of Minnesota and the American University of Judaism. Each of them spent several days teaching and speaking with Beth Jacob congregants. Each taught five times, from Friday night to Sunday morning, through texts of various kinds including Divrei Torah at services and a Shabbat afternoon session

What did the scholars teach? They brought to Beth Jacob the most important scholarship done today in the field of Jewish Studies. They covered the breadth of Judaic learning: Talmud, Hebrew Bible, Midrash, liturgy, poetry, Jewish ethics, Jewish history, and material culture. They explored the Judaism of the ancient, medieval, early modern and contemporary worlds. They taught about the worlds of Ashkenaz and the Levant. I remember in particular the teachings of Dr. Benjamin Gampel, professor of Medieval Jewry and Sephardic History at the Jewish Theological Seminary. He addressed crisis and creativity in the Sephardic world, a subject rich in history but little understood by those of us (like me) who grew up in exclusively Ashkenazi communities. And I recall as well Shaye J.D. Cohen, Harvard professor of Hebrew Literature and Philosophy, whose 1999 book, *The Beginnings of Jewishness, Boundaries, Varieties, Uncertainties,* addressed the boundary between Jews and gentiles, and between Judaism and the surrounding cultures, subjects at the heart of Jewish identity, self-definition and community.

But lest anyone mistakenly believe that the scope of Jewish learning fostered by Harold and Mickey rests solely in the synagogue, or in book learning, or in the wonderful programming Harold and Mickey made possible at Beth Jacob, I want to mention the Harold and Mickey Smith Gallery of Jewish Arts and Culture at the Minneapolis Institute of Arts. That gallery exhibits beautiful objects of Judaica accumulated by Harold and Mickey over the years and donated to the museum for display and learning.

How do I know the gallery is a source of learning? Since my mother injured her shoulder in a fall last year, she has had someone who comes to her apartment to help with chores. The helper is a lovely young Eritrean mother of a second grader. In December, the young mother took her child to the Minneapolis Institute of Arts. They passed the Harold and Mickey Smith Gallery, the child insisted on stopping. "Look," he said, all excited. "Look, there is a menorah!"

This story seems to me the proper bookend for the Smith Scholar in Residence Program. Together, the two acts of generosity demonstrate Harold's dedication to learning and his goal of keeping the community thinking and thriving. I have been lucky to be on the receiving end of that generosity, in the Scholar in Residence Program, at the Minneapolis Institute of Art, and in conversations over coffee and dinner. I have come to admire your intellectual curiosity, your life-sustaining tenacity, and your thoughtful generosity. For all that I am grateful.

So thank you, Harold! And the warmest wishes for very Happy Birthday – and many, many more! I look forward to more wonderful conversations with you.

Love,

Lisa

Lisa Tiegel is a member of Beth Jacob Congregation in Mendota Heights, MN

The Harold and Mickey Smith Gallery of Jewish Arts and Culture

Dr. Evan Maurer

AS A YOUNG art museum director, I was told that one of my main jobs was to "collect" collectors. But when it came to starting a gallery devoted to Judaica, I didn't "collect" Harold, he "collected" me! The Minneapolis Institute of Art (MIA), of which I was the CEO when I got to know Harold, is over 100 years old, so it is appropriate to be celebrating Harold's 100th birthday.

The Institute is among the largest and finest art museums in the country and has a very good reputation for its collections and exhibitions of art from all over the world, from ancient to contemporary. Every major religion and cultural legacy is represented at the MIA. And as we kept building and expanding gallery space during the 1990s and up to 2005 we got new opportunities to show more types of art from around the world.

The one great religious and cultural tradition that wasn't represented at the museum was Judaism and the varied ways the arts were alive for Jews in Israel and countries on every continent. As we increased our gallery space there was one area that was never claimed because it was bisected by a corridor that connected the Main building to the new East Wing and its large special exhibition galleries.

But I saw this as a special opportunity as this crucial avenue would bring more visitors to it then if the gallery was tucked away amidst others.

Up to then the only art museum in the United States with a gallery devoted to Judaica was in Raleigh, North Carolina.

A major goal at the MIA was reaching out to all communities it served in the Minneapolis - St. Paul metropolitan area and throughout the state. We strongly felt that when people learn about other cultures and religions, they are better able to understand and appreciate their values and contributions to world history, and it was time we had a gallery devoted to the culture and art of our large Jewish population here in the Twin Cities.

So now we had a gallery, but we had no collection! That's when I was introduced to Mickey (*zichrona livracha*) and Harold Smith (*she-yibadel lechayim arukim*). My first visit to their home in St Paul was like being with wonderful relatives. Harold and Mickey were warm and welcoming they made me feel like I was visiting *mishpacha* – family. I told Harold about our plans to build a gallery and collection but having no examples to display. That's when Harold took me on a tour of his Judaica collection which was broad and of very fine quality. Harold said that he would be willing to lend the museum works of art from his collection. Very generously, he also promised to donate the largest part of his collection if the museum could create a gallery that would always be devoted to Judaica and Jewish artists.

The only way this could be assured was by endowing funds for the gallery. Harold, Mickey, and I shared a dream that we could make this happen. To my eternal gratitude, Harold and Mickey then made a major contribution to the museum and so the Harold and Mickey Smith Gallery was created, only the second such gallery of Judaica in any American art museum. Because of the Smith's key gift that gallery will always be an integral part of our world class art museum.

We opened the gallery with loans and gifts from Harold's collection and a display of powerful photographs by Robert Frank of Israel during the War of Independence in 1948.

From that moment on the collection was expanded by gifts from others who also believed in Harold and Mickey's goals. A curator was trained at the Institute and in New York City, and assigned to caring for and expanding the collection and to develop exhibitions and public programs. A few years ago, great patrons from Minneapolis created a very substantial purchase fund that allowed our museum to be competitive in acquiring the best works of art available.

The Smith gallery quickly became a very popular attraction and teams of specially trained docents give regularly scheduled educational tours. Jewish visitors admired objects they were familiar with and non-Jewish visitors had a welcomed chance to learn about Judaism and its values which they had read about in their own Bible studies. With understanding comes respect for other people, and for the environment upon which we all depend.

Harold and Mickey made it possible for the Minneapolis Institute of Arts to be a national leader in bringing Jewish arts and traditions to millions of people, both now and in the future. Harold's collection and generosity was a great *mitzvah*, taking its place alongside the Smith's many other generous contributions to Jewish education and life.

Harold's support of and continuing interest in the Jewish art gallery that bears his and Mickey's names is one of the most unique and culturally effective benefactions in the museum's more than 100-year history. Harold, you are an extraordinary man devoted to making a life well spent add to the lives of countless others. You brought alive the ancient Jewish saying *"Le'dor V'dor"* – from generation to generation. You are also the warmest and kindest of friends, projecting an aura of welcome with your enthusiastic voice that makes us all smile.

Dear Harold, working with you has been a great honor and joy and I am ever grateful to be your friend. Congratulations on your century and all you have accomplished. With warm and loving regards!

Evan

Evan M. Maurer, Ph. D. is Director Emeritus of The Minneapolis Institute of Art

Harold with visiting school group at the Harold and Mickey Smith Gallery

The Harold and Mickey Smith Gallery of Jewish Arts and Culture

Honoring Harold's Love of Judaica

Making the Jewish Past Come
Alive at the Israel Museum

Miki Joelson

It was my pleasure to meet Harold at the Israel Museum in Jerusalem during his March, 2017 visit to dedicate the Mickey and Harold Smith Enhancement Center for cancer patients at Hadassah Medical Center in Ein Kerem, opened thanks to the support. of Harold and his late wife Mickey.

WE STARTED OUR TOUR at the Shrine of the Book, looking at the oldest known Biblical scrolls, which were discovered in the Judean Desert. Our tour continued as we headed off to explore the galleries of the Jack, Joseph and Morton Mandel Wing for Jewish Art and Life, displaying material culture from Jewish communities around the world. It was there when I was introduced to Harold and son Mitchell's fascination with the stories and knowledge that lie within every artifact, along with a deep appreciation of their aesthetical value. I learned this was also the spirit behind the collection built by Harold and Mickey during their travels in Israel, Europe and North Africa, featuring Jewish ritual and ceremonial objects, which they donated to the Minneapolis Institute of Art and is displayed there in the Harold and Mickey Smith Gallery of Jewish Arts and Culture.

The Jewish Art and Life Wing in the Israel Museum holds one of the richest and most diverse collections of Jewish material culture in the world, spanning from the Middle Ages to the present day. The collection tells us a lot about differences and similarities in rituals, communal values, materials and artistic influences in each community. In 2010 the Museum was re-inaugurated after a comprehensive renewal project, and the galleries were expanded tremendously, which enabled a wider display of objects from the collection. This also demanded the rethinking of the curatorial concept, a process that culminated in five main galleries dealing with key themes: (1) *The Rhythm of Life: Birth, Marriage, and Death*, presenting objects used for major life passages "highlighting the coexistence of joy and sadness, life and death, memory and hope at each of these junctures in the life cycle;" (2) *Illuminating the Script*, displaying rare illuminated Hebrew manuscripts which "shed light on their artistic importance and their central role in the history of the Hebrew book;" (3) *The Synagogue Route: Holiness and Beauty*, featuring four interiors of synagogues from Europe, Asia and America, along with Torah scroll ornaments and Torah Ark Curtains from Jewish communities around the world; (4) *The Cycle of the Jewish Year*, dealing with "the sanctity of the Sabbath, and the traditional celebration of religious holidays, as well as the new commemoration of special days in the State of Israel;" and last but not least, (5) *Costume and Jewelry: A Matter of Identity*, showing "unique examples of Jewish dress and jewelry, which reflect Jewish identities from East and West, and influenced by the laws and customs of each individual local community." (All quotes are taken from the curatorial gallery texts.)

The display's thematic approach enables a view of each object in various contexts of time and space. It shows sacred and mundane items together, in a way much more like an actual Jewish home, but at the same time, it enhances the comparative view of customs and material manifestations of beliefs and practices between communities around the world.

During our visit, Harold, Mitchell and I had a fascinating conversation on this aspect as we were discussing the role of amulets, which are many times used in the most fragile moments of one's life. We spoke of the different examples that are on display, including amulets for a pregnant woman and a baby, symbolic patterns on wedding garments and a special stone on which a glass was broken under the *huppah*, and noted how people's felt need for protection has been so strong in different places and eras.

In my role as assistant to the Chief Curator of the Jewish Art and Life

Wing I am often intrigued with the question of the various ways available to share with the public the knowledge and history behind the objects in our collection, accumulated through many years of research and fieldwork by generations of curators and scholars.

While this issue lies at the base of every curatorial work, in the past year and a half it has become a key focus in an educational project I have been developing and co-leading with a colleague from the Museum's Youth Wing for Art Education, called *Gateways to Jewish Art and Life at the Israel Museum*. I shared my insights with Harold and Mitchell and discovered this was a challenge we had in common, as a collector, a developer of educational programs for Jewish youth, and a museum curator.

This program aims to enhance the visitor's experience of Jewish art and culture while exploring individual and collective identities. It seeks to spark dialogue about Jewish and Israeli heritage; the multi-faceted nature of Jewish history; and the richness and pluralism of Jewish culture through guided tours for students and a user-friendly smartphone application for independent visitors and families. These leverage the Museum's wealth of artifacts from Jewish cultures around the world in the Wing's permanent display, as well as selected exhibits from the Archaeology and Israeli Art galleries.

So far, over 6,000 students in seventh, eighth, and ninth grade classes have experience the program's curriculum and innovative methods developed especially for this program which aim to enhance their experience in the Museum and to provide them with material they can relate to and engage with. The tours are guided by the experienced staff of the Youth Wing and deal with the following subjects:

Link to the Past: Designed for seventh graders celebrating their Bar or Bat Mitzvah around this time, this tour highlights the connection between the past and the present in Jewish and Israeli culture. Participants encounter artifacts in the Jewish Art and Life Wing, the Archaeology Wing, and the Shrine of the Book. The route deals with such issues as collective memory, Hebrew script, ceremonies marking personal life passages, and Jewish knowledge passed down from generation to generation.

Circles of Belonging: Eighth graders are invited to explore their interpretations of the individual as a part of a community, while learning about personal and communal objects in the Jewish Art and Life Wing and the Israeli Art galleries. The tour aims to help students connect with their heritage, raising open-ended questions such as who they would like to invite to their sukkah, or how they would they envision the ten commandments of their class.

Jewish, Israeli, Both, or Neither?: Ninth graders are challenged to discuss the complexity of their Jewish and Israeli identities and raise questions about what happens when Jewish tradition meets contemporary life. As they visit the Jewish Art and Life Wing and Israeli Art galleries, topics addressed include traditional and secular approaches to Shabbat and ancient symbols in contemporary contexts.

Now in its second year, Gateways tours for school groups have become an integral part of the Youth Wing curriculum, and Youth Wing guides are engaged in sharing their personal connections and interpretations of the program's material.

In November 2017, we also launched a digital smartphone application that offers self-guided and interactive tours in the Jewish Art and Life galleries for individuals and families. The tour takes the participant on a 10-station adventure, shedding light on key subjects in Jewish tradition and culture and providing related images, trivia questions, games, and activities. The app presents themed routes that include *Family Connections* and *From Generation to Generation.* The idea was to introduce a new way to explore the galleries according to thematic cross sections, in a similar way to the guided tours' rationale, and offer another point of view regarding the passing down of traditions as manifested through Jewish material culture. This is implemented through exhibits such as the Exodus from Egypt, the Ten Commandments, family emblems and heirlooms, and objects displaying the roles of family members in Jewish tradition. We hope that in the future, additional thematic tours will be offered.

We hope these two tools will help offer a new way to experience our display and discuss prominent subjects in one's identity, which arise from many of the objects on display.

As I conclude this mere taste of some thoughts regarding the display of Jewish material culture and the means to convey it to the public, it is my pleasure and honor to participate in this festive publication, celebrating Harold's 100 birthday! My heartfelt wishes for Harold, and may you keep enjoying the family and the young generation for many years, and may you continue to support the legacy of love for Jewish heritage and creativity.

With warm wishes,

Miki

Miki Joelson is Assistant Curator of the Jack, Joseph and Morton Mandel Wing for Jewish Art and Life at Jerusalem's Israel Museum

Jewish Education: Our Very Future

Rabbi Alexander Davis

The following is excerpted from Rabbi Davis' Yizkor Sermon on Yom Kippur, 5773

ONCE THERE WAS a man who wanted to build a house. He went to his rebbe and asked for advice. The rebbe who was immersed in his learning put down his Talmud. "This is a most auspicious question," the rebbe said. "Why, right now I'm studying the tractate of the Talmud about houses. Here take the Talmud and follow the directions."

The man went home delighted. He followed the Talmud's directions: four cubits here, six cubits there. A month later he had a beautiful house and he invited the community to a house dedication. But then it came time to put up the mezuzah. He gave it a little tap with the hammer and the entire structure collapsed. Frantic, the man returned to the rebbe. "I don't know what went wrong," he said.

"The Talmud is a holy book," replied the rebbe." It must be studied carefully. Obviously, you were careless. Get yourself a friend and have him read the directions to you and follow them exactly to the letter."

The man went right to work with his friend. This time it took five months as his friend read every direction and he repeated it back. When he finished, again the man invited the entire community to celebrate the dedication of the house. He lifted the hammer to affix the mezuzah and wouldn't you know it, again, the entire house fell down!

This time the man was furious. He went to the rebbe's house and opened the door without knocking. He threw the big volume of the Talmud down on the table in front of the rebbe.

"Again!" the man shouted. "I carefully followed all of the Talmud's directions and it still fell down."

"Hmm." The rebbe studied the appropriate page of the Talmud. "Wait a minute," he finally said. "Rashi asks the same question!"

As we enter the new year of 5773 we take pride in our beautiful new home. We dedicated phase one. We dedicated phase two. We hung two *mezuzot*. Unlike the story, I am not concerned that the physical structure will fall down. But this year, the question we must ask ourselves is, will it remain standing? We completed our L'dor Vador campaign for the building. But the goal was never bricks and mortar. Today we must ensure that our community continues *midor ledor*, from one generation to the next.

And the truth is, the rebbe had it right. Talmud might not help build the house. But it is what will preserve it. For learning is the key to Jewish living. It is the foundation to Jewish community, the fuel for Jewish continuity.

Some of you are probably saying to yourselves: "Study. Of course, *he's* excited by it. He's a rabbi. He just spent four months in Israel. But study is not my thing."

Well it's true. In Israel, I felt like a kid in a candy store with so many opportunities to learn. But I wasn't always this way. I was the kid who wanted nothing to do with my Temple's Sunday school. On Yom Kippur, I confess: "It was me. I had something to do with our fourth-grade teacher quitting mid-year in tears."

I was scarred from religious school days. I think some of you can relate. So I wanted nothing to do with it after my bar mitzvah. But at some point in college, I learned Torah and suddenly, whole new worlds opened up. Torah was not just a window to the past. It was a window on the world, on my life, on my soul. This was the Torah we stay up all night studying on Shavu'ot, the Torah with which we dance on Simhat Torah, the Torah about which we sing, *ki hem ḥayeinu v'oreḥ yameinu* - Torah is our life, and the length of our days.

Unfortunately, that's not how everyone experiences learning. At some point, many years ago across the United States, the Jewish ideal of life-long learning was reduced to memorizing a bunch of skills. The goal of education became performance. Along the way, we outsourced our studies from parents to teachers, from home to school. And we separated learning about Jewish living from living the very life Judaism tries to cultivate. Like a plant without roots, it was only a short step to the conclusion that at 13, we had learned everything there was to learn. Torah had nothing more to teach.

But Torah is not about information. It is about transformation. Information is trivia that's easily forgotten. Transformation leaves a mark on our soul. Educating for information is interesting but it doesn't inspire. Educating for transformation molds our character. This is the message of a midrash on our Torah reading:

"While the Temple exists," God said, "bring sacrifices for atonement. But when the Temple is gone, busy yourself with words of Torah and they will atone for you. *L'hitasek b'Torah hein m'kaprin.*" (Tanḥuma Aharei Mot, 10)

How can Torah study atone for our transgressions? For Jews, learning is not just about acquiring knowledge. It's about transforming our lives. Torah is not a scroll, or a trope, or a story, or history. Torah means "instruction." It is wisdom for living. Being engaged in Torah atones, for – at its best – learning connects our minds, our hearts and our hands. It moves us to more fully encounter ourselves, each other and God. It strengthens us as a community and inspires us to do our part to repair the world by growing in *mitzvot.*

My dream is that Beth El becomes a learning and a learned community. We have to become Shavu'ot Jews, not just Seder Jews; Simchat Torah Jews, not just Shabbat-table Jews. For, if we want to be a light unto the nations, the light of learning must burn within. Hebrew, history, halakha. Musar, Midrash, Mishnah. Talmud, Torah, T'shuvot (Responsa). And on and on. My dream is for our children to love being Jewish. But they can't love it, unless they know it. And they won't love it, unless *you* learn it, *you* live it, *you* love it.

Today we are blessed to live in an amazing age when new technology is revolutionizing how we learn. That my sixth grader is doing most of his school work on a iPad is no longer surprising. But this year my Aleph School child will begin using them as well. I keep expecting one day soon as we start singing "*v'zot haTorah*" to see someone lift aloft an iScroll! Or that rabbis will turn to Help-I-need-a-sermon.com! Clearly, we have more access to learning at our fingertips (literally) than Rambam could have ever dreamed of. And yet open access means little if we are not Googling. We must reclaim the title, "People of the Book" or perhaps, "People of the Nook."

And today is the day to begin. We think of Yom Kippur as a time of forgiveness, of apologies and confessions. And it is all those things. But what really happened on this date? The Israelites received the Torah. Yom Kippur is a second Shavu'ot. Moshe received the Torah on Shavu'ot and subsequently smashed the tablets. On Yom Kippur, he received the second set of tablets. You might say Moshe upgraded to the Tablet 2.0.

What's the difference between the first and second set of tablets?

Just before we read "*Adonai Adonai El raḥum v'ḥanun*," we read in the Torah: "*Vayifsol shnei luḥot avanim* - Moshe carved two tablets." The first set of tablets were carved by God. The second set were carved by Moshe. With the first set, Moshe was a passive recipient. With the second, Yom Kippur set, he was an active participant.

And that is what we need today. It is not enough to pass the Torah down from generation to generation. It must be received anew, accepted in each generation. And it starts with us. "*P'sol lekha – carve* new tablets for yourself," God said to Moshe. "*Psol lekha –* for yourself." They cannot be for future generations unless they are first and foremost for *you*. Moshe didn't drop kids off at Mt Sinai and say, "go learn. I'll pick you up in 40 days." He himself went up the mountain.

Let's say we all agreed that learning is important. Who can afford the time? The truth is, we can't afford not to make the time. We are busy. Our kids are busy. But we must carve out time. Our future as a community and a people depends on it. In the words of British Chief Rabbi Jonathan Sacks, "We are the only nation in history to predicate its survival on education."

And so this year, as we celebrate the opening of our Learning Center, we launch "Beth El Learns." The Center is to be more than a repository of books. It is to be a vital area of activity. I invite you to check out the broad range of programs we are offering: Take a class. Teach a class. Let us host your book group. Start a study group. Find a study partner. Receive weekly *divrei Torah* on line. Watch an on-line class.

Our goal between Simḥat Torah and Shavu'ot is that once a week, every person here engages in Jewish learning of some kind. Torah study is broad enough to encompass all our interests and learning styles as we've tried to reflect in the offerings of "Beth El Learns." And today, it's more convenient than ever before. This is a dream we can achieve.

There are a number of challenges we currently face in our local Jewish education:

First, we must address how we deliver Jewish education. Every week I read about new, creative ideas: home *shuling*, on-line Torah trope trainers, b'nai mitzvah merit badges. I even read about a class that has girls paint scenes of the *parasha* (weekly Torah portion) on their nails! Some of these ideas are worth exploring.

Second, we must address changing learning styles and understand the many demands on our students. That's why I am co-chairing a Minneapolis initiative to reexamine Jewish education for our teen population.

Third, we must address how our teachers are supported and trained. This will be an issue I will raise at the Federation on whose board I sit.

Finally, of course we must address cost. Did you know that every year we have to find $50,000 in our synagogue budget for scholarships for the Aleph School? That's to say nothing of the financial needs of our educational partners – schools, summer camps, college campuses. We need your help supporting Jewish education whether or not you have kids in school because *education is quite simply the future of our community.*

All of those issues are crucial. Beth El and the larger community must address them. But none of them should overshadow the most critical piece of them all – the need for life-long learners. For ultimately, the question is not the cost or time commitment. It's how much we value Jewish education. I am convinced that our challenges will be resolved when and only if, adults love learning. So I need you to share that dream, the dream of children and adults dancing with the Torah and staying up all night studying, the dream of Torah sweetening our lives throughout our lives.

The *Sh'ma* got it right - learning begins at home, *b'shivtekha b'veitekha*. It begins with parents and grandparents who teach by example. It's not about lecturing; it's about leading. It's not about knowing all the answers. It is about prioritizing - about insisting that Jewish education does not end at 13, about insisting that Jewish education is equal if not more important than other extra-curricular activities. *For it is our very future.*

The word for parent in Hebrew is *horeh*, which shares a root with *moreh*, "teacher," which shares a root with Torah, "instruction." *Horeh*. *Moreh*. Torah. The three are inseparable for parents must transmit the wisdom of Torah. And so, if you carry scars from a religious school that colors your opinion of Jewish education, now is the time, cleanse yourself of them. They not only impoverish you to the beauty of our tradition, they poison your children, the next generation.

"*P'sol lekha*," the Torah says. The Torah is "*l'kha*" – for *you* – and must begin with you. It's not about making you a better Jew. It asks your questions, speaks your language, addresses your interests. It's about eternal values, timeless wisdom, deep spirituality. "When I pray, I speak to God," said Professor Louis Finkelstein of the Jewish Theological Seminary. "When I study, God speaks to me."

A few days ago, someone brought me a program from the original dedication of this building. Flipping through it, I recognized many of the names and could picture the excitement they must have felt. But I knew something else. These men and women did more than dedicate an "Activities Building" and later a sanctuary. They dedicated themselves to passing on the traditions of their ancestors to a future generation. And we must do the same. We did not inherit a building nor are we bequeathing a building. We renovated in order to be renewed. We built a building in order to build a community, in order to pass on a heritage, in order to build a soul, *livnot ul'hibanot* as the early Zionists put it – to build and to be built. And it begins with learning.

I watched as construction workers poured the foundation of the Learning Center. And do you know what that foundation is made of? Concrete and dirt. But not just dirt. Before they poured the cement, we buried sacred books in a *geniza*. Our foundation literally is but more importantly figuratively must be Torah.

Throughout these High Holy Days, we pray to be inscribed *b'sefer hayim*, in the Book of Life. The image is not an accident: a Book of Life. There is no living without learning, in the words of our sages, "*Marbeh Torah marbeh hayim* - the more Torah, the more life."

In the new year, we must affirm the words of our *Yizkor* prayer, *avi mori ... imi morati*. Our parents are our teachers. For although at this hour we feel their absence, we also know, that through our learning they will remain ever present.

As we say, *v'hayei olam nata b'toheinu*, life eternal is planted within us when we hold fast to the Torah, our Tree of Life.

Rabbi Alexander Davis is Senior Rabbi at Temple Beth El in Minneapolis, MN

Jewish Day School Education as a Community Priority

Yoni Binus

Below is a d'var Torah that I delivered in 2015 at Temple of Aaron in St. Paul. The reason I wanted to include this in the Festschrift honoring Harold's 100th birthday, is that I believe it addresses Harold's deep passion and support for Jewish education, Day School education in particular. I was asked, for this d'var Torah, to specifically address affordability and accessibility to Jewish Day School education, which Harold has personally worked for decades to address through his own philanthropy, writing, and advice to those of us working to raise funds specifically for this cause.

Harold has also been a vocal advocate for building bridges across the river, connecting the Jewish communities of St. Paul and Minneapolis. This has, as long as I have known him and I'm sure well before that, been his vision for the Twin Cities. Temple of Aaron invited me, the Head of the Heilicher Minneapolis Jewish Day School, to speak on Shabbat morning, at their synagogue in St. Paul. I believe this piece, for all those reasons, speaks to the essence of Harold Smith as a leader, a visionary, and a supporter and advocate for Jewish education and the possibilities of a stronger and more collaborative Twin Cities Jewish community.

Lastly, I would like to thank Harold for being an inspiration to me and to other leaders of this school and across the community. He is a leader by example and a thoughtful and analytical sounding board for many of us who have taken to the field of Jewish education. I wish him the best as he reaches this incredible milestone and all the years beyond. Mazel tov!

JUST A LITTLE OVER a year ago, I had the honor of speaking at the Adath, delivering the dvar Torah as one of our seventh graders became a bar mitzvah. The *parshat hashavuah* that Shabbat was *Vayishlach*. The story, as you may recall, recounts the potentially explosive, but ultimately anti-climactic, reunion between Jacob and Esau, decades after Jacob had stolen his brother's birthright. Jacob fully expected a violent confrontation, and his spies had told him that Esau was prepared for war. On the eve of this potential battle, Jacob wrestles with the angel or messenger who appears before him. The tableau of this struggle is one of the most enduring images and metaphors in Judaism. What Jew, at a very young age, has not wrestled with her or his own faith or practice or family? What generation of Jews has not grappled with the new realities of geopolitics, technology, and demographic shifting? And one can only imagine the deep conflict for those who experienced slavery in Egypt, oppression and expulsion during the Inquisition, or the horrors of the Holocaust. Jacob's confrontation with the messenger leaves him with some minor injuries and new name, Israel. He is also ready for his reunion with Esau. And, instead of war, Jacob receives forgiveness from his brother.

Just as I crossed a river to be here at the Temple of Aaron, you may recall that Jacob also crossed a river in *Vayishlach* to reunite with his brother. At this point, Jacob and Esau have gone their own way and Jacob has had quite a go of things. Four wives, thirteen children, and the loss of his favorite son, Joseph. And in this week's Torah portion, we are happy for Jacob who no longer need mourn his son, as he discovers Joseph is alive and thriving in the land of Egypt.

Equally important here, is the resolution of the story of Joseph and his brothers and the reconciliation between them. Joseph has his youngest brother, Benjamin, held captive and Judah pleads with Joseph, who still has not revealed himself as their brother, to exchange himself, Judah, for Benjamin. This gesture shows Joseph how much his brothers have grown, and he feels they have earned his forgiveness. The big reveal occurs, and word is sent to Jacob that Joseph is alive and, after a long detour, Jacob's family and bloodline are ready again to continue down the path of realizing their destiny as the bearers of God's promise to Abraham and the nation that will be God's people.

A subtle, yet important, philosophical dispute is also addressed in the course of this story. You see, Judah represented one way of carrying out and carrying on the teachings of the Torah, i.e., that those who were chosen should stay among themselves and learn together and, when they would reach such a high level of knowledge and piousness, others in the world would naturally follow. But Joseph embodied interaction with the rest of society, to intermingle in business, politics, finance, and the world of technological advancement. Joseph's emergence as the forgiver and the leader in this narrative can be seen as an endorsement of a philosophical and tactical approach along *his* vision.

When I look at the modern Jewish Day School movement, I think about Judah's approach versus Joseph's. I understand, through our own market research and many non-scientific but anecdotal conversations, that Jewish Day School is often perceived along the lines of Judah's philosophy, yet it operates along the lines of Joseph's. Community Jewish Day School – whether one calls it community or pluralistic or egalitarian, I don't really find the nomenclature nearly as important as the actual mission – is designed to provide a locus for textual, historical, and practical training for young Jews that simultaneously prepares them to be engaged in, contribute to, be leaders in, and lifelong students of a much broader world.

At Helicher, and I'm sure this is true as well at the Talmud Torah of Saint Paul and the Newman School, global competency, technological savvy and safety, critical thinking and problem solving, and empathy for all humankind, are not only taught but also ingrained as core skills which we believe are necessary for successful, happy and confident children and adolescents.

But, I wasn't asked here to merely advertise Day School, I was specifically asked to address affordability of Day School. Affordability. Such a complex and foreboding topic. Can't I just stay up in the clouds and discuss the importance and the excellence of Jewish Day School? I love to talk about that. I mean, I'm a Day school graduate myself.

I guess not.

The first place to look when we discuss affordability is within the community. The Day School movement, when it emerged and flourished, was borne out of the community's desire to strengthen Jewish knowledge and identity, and love and connection to Israel for those growing up in the United States. The Shoah was only a couple decades to our backs and

Israel was a critical rallying point for Jews around the world. Day School was mom and pop. Day school was the child of the community.

Over the years, Day School actually outperformed itself. The combination of second language learning, critical thinking, and an integrated curriculum of life lessons, skills, and values proved to produce students who were exceptional in academic and professional life. Schools across the country became more sophisticated and self-sustaining and the community, as a parent does with its own child, began to see that Day Schools were able to succeed and thrive without their full attention. Federations continued to support many Jewish Schools, thankfully, but amounts of support ebbed and flowed, and mostly ebbed when the economy took a major turn almost ten years ago.

That's when many schools, including our own here in Minnesota, got caught without a safety net. Our operation had become quite sophisticated, but the expense of that sophistication, combined with individual families' decreasing ability to afford it, left us with a gap between our actual cost to educate and the amount that families could pay. Furthermore, we had not been required to market all of our many strengths and excellent outcomes to Jewish families. People simply sent their kids to Day School when it was time to do so. But when price points become significant, different questions are asked and different programs are sought and we, along with many of our Day School cohort around the country, were simply not marketing all those successes and assets that we had assumed people knew – and that other schools, including public schools, had learned to market.

So, now we have worked on messaging and marketing. We have looked at auditing and strengthening our programs; but the affordability question still remains. The community, if it wants Day School education, must find a way to take care of its own and to help fund the programs it needs. The sophistication of the modern Day School can make it a competitive force in the independent school universe, but it means a need for further community funding, well beyond what was needed in the past, to thrive and carry out its mission.

That's one solution and I believe the communities of the Twin Cities recognize that and are doing what they can to raise the funds for school to continue and for scholarships to be substantial and available.

For individual families, this is a much harder process.

First, I think it's critical for families to understand what they are investing in. Jewish Day School is an all-inclusive, immersive approach to securing for their children Jewish knowledge and practice and a Jewish soul. The integrated approach of Day School provides students with skills they will need and call upon not only when they are fifteen or sixteen, but when they are thirty or forty. It can be seen as an investment in a lifetime of living and Jewish growth.

On a more practical level, when it comes down to actual dollars, it's important that families look at their own priorities, potential reliance on some family members for support, and their willingness to openly go through a financial assistance process.

That's an important one; I think families believe they won't receive assistance because, on paper, they make enough money to pay an extra $1200 or $2400 a month. That is simply not the case. For example, at Heilicher, we have a process by which families apply for financial assistance through a national website which helps calculate reasonable expense against assets and salaries, but it also asks for families to input what they believe they can afford and what other factors may be involved. This is a key part of the allocation process and it's designed to capture families' real situation on the ground and to ensure that families are also able to do those things that families love to do and need to do to get the most out of life AND still invest in Day School education. It's merely the beginning of a dialogue.

This isn't to say that affording Day School won't be a challenge. This isn't to say that there won't be sacrifice involved. I go back to thinking about Jacob and his wrestling with the messenger. *Being Jewish, passing along Judaism, will always be an obligation for individual Jews and each generation of Jews to wrestle with.* That tension is partly what makes our people and our tradition so great. That struggle keeps us sharp and strong and diverse.

For families with very young children, I recommend having discussions now with the leadership of any Day School you are considering. Even if kindergarten is two or three or four years away, those discussions can help you lay the groundwork for setting budgets, savings, and expectations. Those conversations will help you realize that affordability is not an abstract concept but rather an attainable goal, even as you begin the journey of a young family and experience all the expenses that come with that journey.

I was thinking about how relevant it seems that I spoke last year on Jacob's reconciliation with his brother and this year on the *parashah* detailing his son Joseph's reconciliation with his brothers. What we pass down to the next generation can be intended or it can be unintended. Those who started the Day School movement, those who believed in it, and those who perpetuate it, all know that there are unintended inheritances we pass along to our children, and they all, across the board, fundamentally believe that a Jewish Day School education is a way to pass along a powerful, sustaining, and intentional legacy to their children and their children's children. It is now our job to continue that work by partnering to insure the affordability of a Day School education today and well into the future.

Yoni Binus is Head of School, Heilicher Minneapolis Jewish Day School

The Impact of Jewish Day School and Jewish Camping, Part 1

Ethan Kadet

AS I GRADUATE high school and will soon move on to college, I have been reflecting on two parts of my life that impacted me the most. These have been my time at Heilicher Minneapolis Jewish Day School and at Herzl camp. I started going to Heilicher in second grade and made close friends and memories there that I will have for my whole life. The Jewish experiences I had and lessons I learned impact the way I act and treat others today, even if I don't think about it on a daily basis. Some of my best memories at Heilicher were playing on the basketball team with my friends, traveling to Washington, DC with my 8th grade class, and participating in the yearly math competition. Although I might not have thought about it at the time, the Jewish discussions and debates that we had about the Torah and current events have shaped the way I see the world and have made me a more thoughtful person.

I have gone to Herzl camp for eight summers and will be returning this summer for my first year on staff. I believe that the combination of my experiences at Heilicher and Herzl have shaped who I am both as an active member of the Jewish community and as a person. Today, I apply the lessons I learned at Heilicher on being a *dugma*, a role model, to my role as a counselor at Herzl camp, a teacher at my synagogue, and an assistant coach on the Heilicher basketball team.

After I graduated from Heilicher in 8th grade, I chose to play a bigger role in my Jewish community because Judaism was no longer a part of my school day. I chose to participate in out-of-school Hebrew classes, a class on Israel advocacy, USY, and to teach Torah reading at my synagogue. And when I move on to college next year I am excited to find my place in a new Jewish community.

When I was in my final year as a camper at Herzl, I was not excited when I found out my cabin assignment on the first day. I was put with a couple good friends, but I was left out of the cabin that had my larger group of friends with whom I had bunked every year at camp up until then. At first, I was very upset and was hoping that it wouldn't ruin what I had been told was going to be the best summer yet. By the end of the summer my entire mindset had changed. I not only became closer with a few good friends in my cabin, but I learned the important life skill of working with new people and being flexible. Most of my cabin was not from Minnesota and many of them I had never interacted with before that summer. I came away from camp knowing how to better work with and relate to others. For example, a lot of days some of my cabin mates wanted to play cards or chess, when I wanted to go play sports. I learned to adapt and to have a good attitude and have fun in whatever I am doing, whether that was learning a new card game or playing basketball. I have used this lesson of inclusion and being flexible to change many times when working on projects in school, and I will continue to use it in college and in future jobs.

Last summer, as an *Ozo* (counselor-in-training) I really enjoyed teaching Jewish lessons and being able to get younger kids excited about learning new ideas and applying them to their lives at camp and at home. Because of my time at Herzl and Heilicher I have the skills to incorporate my Jewish knowledge in any situation, and to pass down the lessons I learned to the next generation of Jewish leaders.

Ethan Kadet recently graduated from Hopkins High School, where he was a member of the school's ultimate frisbee team and will head to Washington University in St. Louis in the fall of 2018. He attended Heilicher Jewish Day School for seven years and the summer of 2018 marks his ninth year at Herzl Camp.

Im Tirtzu Ein Zo Agadah

Herzl Camp: Molding Jewish Lives

Holly Guncheon

IN THE LATE 1990s, a renaissance began in Jewish camping. In 1998, the Foundation for Jewish Camp was launched, as a national organization dedicated to building a strong Jewish future through transformative summer camp experiences. The publication of *How Goodly are Thy Tents* by Amy Sales and Leonard Saxe in 2000 provided much-needed proof that Jewish camping had a measurable effect on future participation in the Jewish community. In 2004, New England philanthropist Harold Grinspoon established the Harold Grinspoon Institute with the express purpose of incentivizing Jewish camps around the country to develop their fundraising capacity and to invest in their facilities.

These developments began a trend nationwide. Philanthropic dollars began to flow to Jewish camps. Dilapidated camps began rebuilding and expanding their facilities. Beds began to fill, and scholarship funds began to grow.

Meanwhile in the Twin Cities, the work of Mickey and Harold Smith continued, unchanged. Many decades before Jewish camping was "discovered," Harold and Mickey had astutely identified Jewish education - both formal *and informal* - as their philanthropic focus. They had seen the effects of a quality formal and informal Jewish education in their own family as well as the community around them. They put their charitable dollars to work at Herzl Camp as well as their volunteer time, serving on the board and fundraising committees.

As the nation was discovering Jewish camping, Harold and Mickey were quick to seize the opportunity, offering Herzl Camp a $250,000 donation *if* Herzl could match it with donations from new donors. Harold and Mickey's visionary offer was a catalyst for significant change. The board of directors made giving a top priority. They organized committees, hired consultants and eventually staff to drive this new venture into intentional fundraising. All along, Harold and Mickey cheered the volunteers' work at every stage: offering advice, soliciting friends and writing handwritten thank you notes to each new donor. Their efforts, coupled with the national focus, transformed Herzl Camp in just a few short years.

The Smiths' dedication over six decades was proven to be well-placed by the research that began with *How Goodly are Thy Tents* in 2000. Jewish camping was demonstrated to influence future Jewish participation in meaningful ways. Participating in one 3-week session of Jewish camp as a child increased several measures of Jewish identity and involvement.

Individuals who were campers are:

- 21% more likely to feel that being Jewish is important than non-campers
- 37% more likely to light Shabbat candles regularly
- 10% more likely to marry a Jewish spouse
- 55% more likely to feel very emotionally attached to Israel

Their increased commitment to Judaism is evident in their engagement with the Jewish community: Individuals who were campers are:

- 26% more likely to be members of a synagogue
- 45% more likely to attend synagogue at least once a month
- 30% more likely to donate to a Jewish federation or Jewish cause

Jewish camping's critical role in the ongoing creation of a vibrant Jewish community is now broadly recognized and has invigorated the field. Programs to deepen the skills and knowledge of camp boards, camp directors and camp staff abound. Expertise has been leveraged to create better quality curriculum and teaching models for Jewish and Israel education in a camp setting. Efforts to expand the reach of Jewish camp to more children have spawned numerous Jewish specialty camps focusing on sports, arts, outdoors, technology, and many other interest areas. The role of Jewish day camps as critical feeders for overnight camps as well as important informal Jewish education institutions has been recognized more recently with significant dollars and expertise flowing to day camps as a result.

Harold continues to challenge himself to learn new things. As Jewish camping continues to evolve and grow, Harold has also continued to grow and evolve in his work at Herzl Camp. He joined the Herzl Camp Foundation board and is an active solicitor. When he learned of campers' growing interest in specialty cooking camps, he helped to initiate the idea of – and then fund - Mickey's Kitchen (aka Mickey's *Mitbach*) a teaching kitchen named for Mickey, a consummate homemaker.

Just after Mickey's Kitchen opened in 2017, Harold visited camp and participated in a *chug* (activity session) making potato kugel with a group of 10-year old boys.

The Smiths were pioneers in camping philanthropy and Harold continues to lead the way even as he enters his eleventh decade!

Holly Guncheon is the Director of Development of Herzl Camp, located in Webster, WI with offices in Minneapolis, MN

Harold and Mickey at Herzl

In 2015, Harold offered the following at a gathering marking Herzl Camp's 70th anniversary

"With apologies to Abe Lincoln...

Three score and ten years ago, our elders brought forth into the woods of Wisconsin, a new camp, dedicated to the proposition that all Jewish children deserve a meaningful summer camp experience in a totally Jewish setting.

We are met here now to enhance and strengthen the work they so ably started. It is altogether fitting and proper that we should do this.

The world will little note, nor long remember, what we say here, but it can never forget what they accomplished in these last few years.

And so it is incumbent on us, their heirs, to continue their work so that an outstanding Herzl Camp, of the kids, by the kids, and for the kids, shall not perish from the shores of Devils Lake."

Entrance to Herzl camp (top), Herzl campers enjoying
a cooking *chug* in Mickey's Kitchen

Our Love Affair with Herzl Camp

Jake and Marissa Smith

OUR TIME AT HERZL brought us together and has shaped our lives. To say that it has influenced us would be an incredible understatement. We know that without Herzl Camp we would not be where we are today.

As campers, we both experienced Herzl in similar ways. We were told about what to expect when we got off the buses in Webster from our parents but didn't understand it until we were actually there.

Herzl introduced us to new people, new traditions, and a new way to celebrate being Jewish. It helped us learn self-reliance, independence, and social awareness. But beyond learning those lifelong skills as campers and as staff members, what Herzl gave us was *kehilah*, a community.

Our story started at Herzl. We met as *ozrim* (counselors-in-training) in the summer of 2003. We took walks around Ozo Park. We knew it was serious when we sat with each other at the Shabbat table on Friday nights.

When we got married in 2013, our wedding party was entirely made up of former Herzl campers and staff. We know that any future children of ours will go to Herzl and we will be living vicariously through them.

Even though we are past our days as campers and staff, Herzl continues to shape our lives. The values and culture we learned at Camp have led us to bring Jewish traditions into our home, support Jewish causes, and take on leadership roles in our community.

Thankfully, the positive impact of Herzl on our lives is not unique. Countless individuals have their own meaningful memories, and campers and staff continue to make new memories every summer.

Harold and Mickey's philanthropy has ensured the next generation will have the same (and better!) opportunities to experience Herzl Camp. We love talking about and visiting Herzl with Harold, it is such a special bond that we share. Happy 100th birthday, Harold!

Jake Smith, Harold's great nephew, is the grandson of Harold's brother Marvin, zichrono livracha. Jake's wife Marissa is a member of the Herzl Camp Board of Directors.

Dedication plaque for the dining hall at Herzl Camp

Herzl

By Lucy Schwartz

Herzl is a fun and amazing camp. I love Herzl in many ways. I make so many friends and there are the best activities at Herzl. I learn so much about being Jewish. Here are some of the things I love the most about Herzl.

Home. I am always happy at Herzl. It's my home away from home. Herzl is my favorite camp. I can't wait to go this summer.

Every single day. Every day at Herzl is so much fun. All the activities are great and lots of fun. One of my favorites is planting in Margie's garden.

Ruach. I love all the Ruach going on at camp. It's super fun to yell, dance, sing and scream at breakfast.

Zoning out. I love to be active, but peaceful and quiet activities are fun too. For example yoga, quiet time in the cabins, reading time and art.

Laughing with friends. I love Herzl mostly because of all the new friends you can make. I make so many friends from other states that I would not have met if it weren't for Herzl.

Look, that spells Herzl!
These are the reasons why I love Herzl!

Lucy Schwartz is Harold's great great niece

June Schwartz is Harold's great great niece

The Impact of Jewish Day School and Jewish Camping, Part 2

Abigail Yousha

AS AN EIGHT-YEAR-OLD, I climbed the stairs to the coach bus bringing me to sleepaway camp. I rode the bus with girls who shared my excitement to be going away for our first time. Two short hours flew past. I watched excitedly as the bus zoomed past the Burnett Dairy Farm. My enthusiasm built as we passed the beach on Devil's Lake. Finally, my anticipation reached an all-time high as the Herzl Camp sign came into view. As the bus rounded the corner onto Mickey Smith Parkway, the staff on the bus stood up, "Alright, campers. On the count of three: one, two, THREE!: *Here's to dear old Herzl ...*" and the song continued. The busses stopped, and the fledgling campers, who had never in their lives been away from home, timidly, yet eagerly, stepped off the bus. We were greeted by young staff members whose smiles spread wide across their faces, which made it seem as though nobody could possibly be happier. We stepped into the building to an eruption of noise and song by the staff lined along the perimeter to welcome us into camp.

This was my first taste of Herzl Camp, and it has stuck with me ever since. I come back every summer and experience the same anticipation as the bus rounds the corner. I am greeted every year with an explosion of welcoming cheers and spirit. This past summer, I gave this experience to my own campers. I returned for my ninth summer at camp as a staff in training (*Ozo*), with the strong desire to spread the Herzl magic to my own campers while strengthening my relationships with other staff members.

That was my first taste of camp, but this doesn't explain why I've returned every summer since 2008.

Camp taught me independence, changed my view of the world, and strengthened my values. I've grown into the 18-year-old I am today by using my independence at camp to evolve my social skills to be socially successful in any setting I'm in. Being assigned to a cabin with girls I don't know, yet in a welcoming community of campers my age, has helped me to communicate and make friends. I've changed from an awkward child and have grown into a person with considerable communication skills. In order to get along with the thirteen other campers living with me, I have learned to be able to make compromises, work as part of a team, and communicate effectively.

Part of camp life is being given certain responsibilities. We have to set and clean the tables at meals, keep our clothes and bed organized, clean our cabins, and arrive at all meals and activities on time. Any responsibilities demand time management, teach organization skills, and require taking accountability for meeting these responsibilities. I now have obtained these skills and have grown into a person who can create a schedule and manage her time, a person who is organized in her academic and personal life, and a person who understands the scope of her priorities and responsibilities and the importance of taking ownership for them.

This summer I am coming back to camp for my ninth summer. One might ask why I always come back. I continue to return to Herzl Camp every summer because camp has transformed me throughout these many summers to a person with acquired skills and knowledge that are essential not only in the camp bubble in Webster, Wisconsin, but also in the real world where my choices affect the life I live. I have grown into an independent young woman who can communicate effectively, make her own choices, and accept responsibility for those choices.

Beyond this, my years as a student at Heilicher Minneapolis Jewish Day School created a receptivity to the Jewish atmosphere at Herzl. Heilicher 1 gave me a solid education in Torah and Jewish history. My Hebrew studies at HMJDS inspired me to continue my Hebrew education even after I entered public high school. I took CIS (College in the School) Hebrew through the University of Minnesota, and thanks to the Hebrew education I received at Heilicher, I am now beginning college with 15 Hebrew language credits.

Abigail Yousha attended Heilicher from kindergarten through seventh grade and recently graduated from Hopkids High School where she was captain of the girls' ultimate team. She served on the USY regional board and will be attending Tulane University in the fall of 2018.

The Values of Spiritual Peoplehood: A Reconstructionist Approach to Jewish Camping

Rabbi Jeff Eisenstat

In 2001 I was invited to help create a Jewish Camp run by the Jewish Reconstructionist Federation (JRF) to embody the vision of the founder of Reconstructionist Judaism, Rabbi Mordecai Kaplan, an early proponent of Jewish summer camps. As founding director, I looked to expand upon work in Kaplan's educational values done by my Reconstructionist colleagues Rabbis Jeffrey Schein and Jacob Staub, and further developed these "Values of Spiritual Peoplehood" to be the philosophical foundation of this Reconstructionist Camp JRF, now known as Camp Havayah.

Khokhmah (Wisdom) takes us to texts both ancient and modern as we delve into the style and methodology of learning that is steeped in our Jewish tradition. As Reconstructionists we have engaged in this study in formal ways, but there is an added excitement as we make the text come alive with innovative and creative activities. It has always been our duty to examine texts and hear the words and thoughts spoken to us from each period (what Kaplan referred to as each civilization) of Jewish life, and in each culture where Jews lived and expressed themselves.

Although there is one specific time during our camp day that embraces learning which we call *havayah* (experience) we take advantage of any opportunity that presents a Jewish teachable moment. Traditional texts are always an essential starting point, but opportunities for experiential learning are to be found in modern, whether in poetry, song, American or Hebrew, folk or pop, or stories of our heritage of any other culture.

Hiddur Mitzvah (literally: enhancement or beautification of the *mitzvah*, here taken as **Creativity**) reminds us of a time in our observant past when the visual arts could be used only in beautifying a *mitzvah*, resulting in centuries' worth of adorned ritual objects. *Menorot* and *kiddush* cups, wimples and *tallitot, mizrahs* and *ketubot*, Torah mantels and Shabbat table cloths were all beautiful ways to enter into the world of art. It is now our joyous task to open these avenues and many more roads to informal learning, enhancing the connection to our heritage in the modern and ancient world.

At Camp JRF we use all forms of art, including drama, music, drums, dance, glass making, wood shop, fabric, yarn, etc. to be the medium for creativity. When campers write plays or songs that reflect the values of camp and then build the backdrops and build the lighting system, it all falls into our understanding of *hiddur mitzvah*.

Kedushah (literally: holiness, here taken as **Spirituality**) takes us to a different realm – one in which we can encounter the Divine. For many, prayer has been offered as the first step in finding a spiritual connection, but it need not be the only path. Community expression, nature and the environment, music and meditation, rhythm and dance – all these vehicles can have a mystical approach for the individual and the group. It is an essential (yet not always easy) journey to find that spiritual chord.

In an entry from his diary, Kaplan wrote about his utter dismay when visiting his daughter Judith at camp in the 1920s and observing children praying without any *kavvanah* (meaning or intention) in their assembly. I read this passage to our own campers and they said that Rabbi Kaplan would have a very different opinion observing the meaningful intentional approach our camp has towards prayer and spirituality.

Ziyonut (Zionism, here taken as **Peoplehood**), which might better be known by the less "political" term *Am Yisrael* (the Jewish people), signifies the connection of the Jewish people to the land and the people of Israel through language, culture and heritage. As Reconstructionists we feel the connection to cultural Zionism, but we also attempt to be sensitive to ways in which the children of Isaac and the children of Ishmael can be brothers and sisters in a world of peace.

Over the past years at Camp JRF we have had a most successful *Mishlahat* (delegation of Israeli staff) that has helped infuse our camp with Hebrew language, culture, politics, and most significantly a heightened sense of Peoplehood. It is not unusual for us as North Americans and Israelis to discuss and debate with our own socio-political values what the essential commonalities and differences are among and between us, and what the role of the land and people of Israel might be. A strong emphasis over the past years has developed as we send our rising 11th graders to Israel for a month which begins and ends at camp, so our younger campers can be excited and impacted by this important pilgrimage.

Tikkun Olam (Repairing the World) makes us ask the question, "How can we as Jews and as human beings bring about a better world?" There can be no doubt that we should incorporate into our lives a sense of *tzedek* – social, political, and economic justice – and a vision of working towards mending our universe, both locally and globally.

For urban and suburban children camp has always been a way to get out into the country and away from the hustle of daily city life. But a new era of environmental concerns have energized and enabled our staff and campers to recycle, compost, plant our own food, green our own camp, and take to the woods with zero impact camping. *Teva* (nature) has become a topic of greater interest in the 21st century, and camp strives to be an important factor in environmental education.

In Pirkei Avot 1:2, Rabbi Simon the Just taught: *Al shelosha devarim haolam omed ...* The world rests on three things: Torah (study), Service/Worship, and Acts of Loving Kindness" Perhaps we need to reclaim *Avodah* as Service – dedication to the world outside of ourselves. In our first year at Camp JRF we realized we did not have a space for an outdoor sanctuary and in six days our entire camp built with holy service a *Beit Tefillah* (House of Prayer) and on the seventh day we sanctified

gave a rabbi a partial wig to enable him to keep his illness from his congregants.

For one patient, at least, the Center has proven not only life-enhancing, but undisputedly life-saving. She is a young woman who grew up hearing the horrors of her mother's concentration camp incarceration. For her mother, the shaving of her long, beautiful hair had symbolized everything she suffered, and her daughter refused any treatment that would make her bald. She agreed to chemotherapy only when she learned of the Center's hair-gluing technique.

> *"My mother was taken to a concentration camp as a teenager. One of the first things they did to her there was shave off her long and beautiful hair. Of all the horrors she experienced, that seemed to symbolize everything for her. That was the one thing she constantly talked about. I grew up with her story. And I can't put myself in treatment that will make me as bald as she was."*

The sophisticated treatment promised by major medical centers conjures images of linear accelerators, cardiovascular intervention and organ transplantation. All are available at Hadassah, but so too are vital tools for the patient's emotional well-being, approaches that bolster confidence and self-esteem, and upgrade daily life. Prominent among these interventions is the Smith Enhancement Center. It is Mickey and Harold's tribute to their daughter Marjorie, who sought without success a suitable wig when undergoing her own chemotherapy, and a living testimony of their desire to help others during desperate times in their lives.

> *"Of course, tears come to my eyes with thoughts of Margie and how with these few dollars we are giving a little happiness to these people who are suffering so."*
> Mickey Smith, September 16, 2009

Neither Mickey nor Harold ever let anything deter them from their goal. When they came to Israel for the 2008 Cornerstone mission, the two of them participated in all the activities. It was amazing but exhausting.

Meeting with the prime minister, flying in a helicopter, and many more activities. Most people planed a relaxing day, a day at the spa or a flight back for the morning after. But not Harold and Mickey; they wanted to come and spend the morning with us at the Enhancement Center - to meet the doctors, the care team, and see the place and the people it serves. Mickey said that that visit was the highlight of her trip. They were indeed צנועי לכת, נחושים ובעלי לב רחב - humble, determined and big-hearted.

Of the many projects that you, Harold, with your dear Mickey, have embraced, the Smith Enhancement Center at Hadassah is perhaps the clearest expression of your love for the Jewish people and humankind, and the way in which you have always acted on that love. It speaks more clearly than any words of a shared life spent making the world a better place, by reaching out to individuals, body and soul. Your energy for making a difference has never flagged over many decades, and your devotion and dedication seem to increase with every year.

The establishment and the impact of the Smith Enhancement Center is truly a testimony to Mickey and the importance she placed on helping people feel better – both physically and emotionally – at a very difficult time in their lives. We can't think of a more significant expression of who she was and what she believed in.

Mickey once said that helping was her privilege, to which you responded that being her husband was your privilege. Let us add that our privilege has been to know you and Mickey. It is the shared privilege of Hadassah, of Israel and of every one of the hundreds of patients helped there. Each one of us is richer for having you in our lives.

Happy 100th birthday! Sending our love and best wishes.

Professor Shlomo Mor-Yosef
Director General (2001 – 2011)
Hadassah Medical Organization

Osnat Moskowitz
Director of Development 2001–2010)
Hadassah Medical Organization

The Mickey and Harold Smith Enhancement Center was established after the Smiths of St. Paul, Minnesota lost their daughter Marjorie to cancer at the age of 30. Marjorie was a very sociable young woman and during her chemotherapy treatment there were no suitable wigs or other means to help her maintain her confidence and self-esteem.

Mickey Smith, who would later lose her own battle with cancer, felt that something needed to be done so that other cancer patients would not have to go through that problem alone, and as a long-time member of Hadassah, pushed for the establishment for this Center. Marjorie always took joy in being of service to others, and the Smiths honor Marjorie's legacy through the daily work of this Center.

המרכז לשיפור איכות החיים שנוסד על ידי מיקי והרולד סמית', עוזר בין השאר במימון פאות וטיפולים קוסמטיים עבור מטופלי מכון שרת. המרכז הוקם לאחר שבני הזוג סמית' מסנט פול, מינסוטה, שכלו את בתם מרג'ורי, שנפטרה מסרטן בגיל 30. מרג'ורי הצעירה הייתה חברותית מאד, ובמהלך הטיפולים שעברה לא היו בנמצא פאות מתאימות או דרכים אחרות לסייע לה בשמירה על תחושת הערך והביטחון העצמי.

מיקי סמית', שאף היא התמודדה עם מחלת הסרטן, חשה שיש לפעול כדי שחולי סרטן נוספים לא יצטרכו להתמודד עם הבעיה לבדם. כחברה ותיקה בארגון נשות הדסה היא פעלה ללא ליאות להקמת המרכז. מרג'ורי שמחה תמיד לחיות לעזר לאחרים, ודרך פעילותו היומיוסית של המרכז, משפחת סמית' מכבדת את מורשתה.

The Mickey and Harold Smith Enhancement Center (top) and Dedication Plaque

Mickey and Harold with Israeli Prime Minister Ariel Sharon
Hadassah Mission, 2008

Remembering Mickey

Whoso findeth a good wife, findeth a great good and obtaineth favor of the Lord

Proverbs 18:22

Dorothy Lipschultz

I MET MICKEY MAINS fall quarter 1942 at the U when I pledged SDT. We became good friends and I was invited to her and Harold's wedding on a hot sunny Independence Day, July 4, 1943. Mickey looked beautiful in her long-sleeved high neck off-white satin wedding gown. Harold looked equally handsome in his dress Navy whites.

Over the next few years we were busy having children, lots of phone calls about everything and nothing, and the beginnings of our involvement in the community.

When I came home after my first, Tom, was born, Mickey brought dinner over: sweet and sour meet, rice and green beans. I still use that recipe till today!!

Mickey couldn't resist showing me her ever-growing stash of fabrics, and I remember the wringer-style wash machine that she held on to even after getting an automatic because the wringer did a better job with some of the items.

Mickey ran the household which included getting needed maintenance help for various problems that came up around the house, bemoaning my own good fortune since my husband, Tim, could fix just about anything.

In those days we all played cards and formed "minyans" through Hadassah which helped to raise money. We eventually became a foursome – Mickey, me, and my two sisters-in-law Betty Joy Lipschultz and Maidee Golden. Mickey was made an honorary member of the Lipschultz clan.

Once the children were older and better able to care for themselves, the four of us decided we deserved to have a weekend all to ourselves. After stocking the freezers and refrigerators with enough food for our families and our poor dear husbands, we took off to a local motel in the suburbs. No errands to run or meals to cook, no beds to make … a pool at which to sit and sun … and mostly we played mah jong and canasta from first thing in the morning and well into the evening. Back home on Sunday evening, well rested and satiated with cards. This was our custom once a year for quite a few years.

Mickey was a talented seamstress; I could always turn to her for a fix-up job when the situation required it. Over the years we shared so many things, and it was nice to see how our group all got along so well, the wives and the husbands.

Each year, I am always aware when March 29ᵗʰ comes around – that was Mickey's birthday.

Dorothy Lipschultz, her husband Tim, Tim's brother Mel and wife Betty Joy and sister Maidee (Lipschultz) Golden and her husband Morrie were lifelong friends of Harold and Mickey's spanning some seven decades.

Lorita Jacobson

I am happy to remember Mickey as we celebrate Harold's 100ᵗʰ birthday. I still miss her as my thoughts go back to happy times with Mickey, Harold, and my husband Jay. We all respected how much Mickey cared for Hadassah and Herzl Camp. She will always be remembered by campers, parents and other visitors, as they enter Herzl on Mickey Smith Parkway.

Jay and I had a chance to visit the Mickey and Harold Smith Enhancement Center at Hadassah Medical Center and got a VIP tour which Harold arranged for us. We were so impressed with it. What a joy it brings to the people they serve.

I suppose my favorite story is how Mickey left Harold with instructions about how to manage. Till this day I often hear him say "Mickey said to do this" or "Mickey said to do that." And whatever Mickey said, Harold does to this day!

Lorita Jacobson and her late husband Jay, the former Director of Development at the Sholom Home in Minnesota, were longtime friends of Harold and Mickey after meeting through mutual friends, and neighbors in both Minneapolis and Boca Raton.

Laura Epstein

Thirteen years ago, my husband Eppy and I began spending our winters in Florida. We were indeed fortunate to find a condo directly across the hall from Mickey and Harold. One couldn't ask for better neighbors who soon became dear friends.

I learned a great deal from Mickey. She was talented in so many ways, sewing, cooking, etc. Just name it and she could do it. We often enjoyed a hearty laugh together and it was a delight being in her company. Together with Harold, through their philanthropy, they supported numerous causes and helped so many. What a dynamic duo. We miss you, Mickey, but you are forever in our thoughts and our hearts.

As for Harold, he can't cook quite like Mickey did, but he is managing rather well as he turns 100. Not many folks at his age are still playing golf, getting out for cards, driving occasionally and attending numerous events, lectures, etc. Every Shabbat he attends services and Eppy enjoys accompanying him frequently. For my husband it is a highlight of the week.

Harold, the amount of knowledge you have retained is amazing! But dealing with the new technology is another story!! You and I are both trying to keep up with 21st century advances – let's just keep on going!

Mazel tov on this momentous occasion and our best wishes to you always. May we celebrate many, many happy returns together.

Love,

Laura and Eppy

Laura Epstein and her husband Alvin (Eppy) Epstein are Harold's neighbors in Boca Raton.

... and Margie

Wendy Fox

MARGIE AND I were friends since the third grade. Our mothers hooked us up because we were both stamp collectors. We had a quirky little stamp club with a couple of other girls and we usually met at Margie's house. Margie never cared much for the business of working on our stamp collections. She much preferred goofing around, so I never came home from stamp club having accomplished much, but I always came home having had a good time. I remember when Margie and her family took a trip to Canada. She brought each of the stamp club members a folder with Canadian stamps in it as a souvenir. Margie distributed the folders and said, "That's enough for the stamp club for today."

I recall going to Talmud Torah with Margie as her "guest." We must have been in the 5th grade. Margie was so smart that she didn't have to pay much attention in order to master the material, and she didn't. She would talk and whisper and giggle and I thought Hebrew School was much more fun at the Talmud Torah than the Hebrew School I went to at Mount Zion. It wasn't that her Hebrew School was more fun. It was that Margie was at this Hebrew School. Margie was the fun.

Many years later, when we joined SDT sorority at the University of Minnesota together, our friendship really solidified. On any given Saturday night our freshman year, if neither of us had a date, which, that year, was most Saturday nights, Margie would ask me to help her as a member of the "meet and greet" committee. Margie and I would stand inside the front door of the sorority house and when a young man came to pick up his date, we would open the door, show the young man in and greet him saying, "We are the meet and greet committee. Who are you here to pick up? Please sit down and we will get her for you." Then, we would send the couple off on their date wishing them a pleasant evening. Nobody but Margie could have convinced me to do something so silly, yet I loved every minute of it.

Everything I did with Margie was fun because Margie was so high spirited and so much fun to be around. With her curly strawberry blonde hair and sparkling eyes, she made me smile just to look at her. She was popular, bright and energetic and she had the most wonderful, creative sense of humor. Many evenings at the sorority house we would sit in her room in our matching flannel nightgowns, she insisted that we buy matching nightgowns when we were on a shopping spree one day, and we would talk about what Margie termed the "teen traumas" that various sorority sisters were facing. Margie would hold court in her room, as a group of girls would gather, listening while she gave out advice, some serious, most just plain humorous.

We did a lot of singing at the sorority house. Margie had a horrible singing voice and she, I believe, purposely sang loud so that everybody could enjoy and appreciate how horrible her voice was. When we would gather for Monday meetings, whoever initiated the singing would always say, "And now we will sing the sorority song and Margie will remain quiet." Margie loved this. She would smile and sing as loud as she could, making all of us laugh. She was a bit like Lucille Ball in the television show I Love Lucy.

After Margie got cancer, we started talking more about what she called, "adult dilemmas" and we wondered why we were so naïve as to think that our teen traumas were anything worth spending time on. I remember when we were 30 years old and Margie was very ill, and I was going through a difficult divorce. I would call Margie in Washington D.C. to see how she was doing. She never wanted to talk about herself. She always wanted to know how I was doing and she always ended up making me laugh by saying something totally absurd about my situation.

I will always remember Margie as the popular, pretty, peppy, super-smart girl with the curly hair and the sparkling eyes and the personality that energized a room.

After Margie's passing, Mr. and Mrs. Smith and I made it a point to stay in touch. I had always felt close to them because I spent a lot of time at Margie's house over the years. I remember Mrs. Smith, in her saddle shoes, working away on her sewing machine making suits and ties for Mr. Smith while Margie and I played in the basement or in her room. I remember Mr. Smith coming home from work and greeting us with some funny remark and a loving smile. As time went on, Mrs. Smith and I made sure to schedule at least one lunch every summer and one during the school year. One time, Mrs. Smith asked me if she could come with me to pick up my son, Todd, at his daycare center. With my mom gone, and Margie gone, I think that experience was a very special one for both of us. It is one that I will always remember fondly.

After Mrs. Smith passed away, I started spending more time with Mr. Smith. My husband, Jeff, often asked me, "What do you and Mr. Smith talk about when you get together?" I told Jeff that he should join us sometime and see. Jeff did just that and from then on, the three of us have been getting together in the summer, either at our house or at a casual restaurant for a nice relaxing dinner and a long, long, chat. Jeff and I are in awe of the stories that Mr. Smith tells us. He tells stories of his past in great detail and stories of his recent travels and his adventures in Florida. Then, of course, there are the political conversations. Jeff and I are amazed that Mr. Smith reads as many papers as he does each day and that he remembers every detail of every article he reads. We have tried to catch him on detail recollection a couple of times by checking things on Google, and he is never wrong! The number of Jews in Peru? He knows it. The average temperature in Jerusalem in January? He knows it. We so enjoy every minute that we are blessed with his company. He holds a very special place in our hearts.

Mr. Smith (he keeps telling us to call him Harold, but we just can't) is amazing and, we hope to make many more happy memories with him in the future.

I must add a fun fact here. Mr. Smith has coupons taped to the inside of his apartment door for any restaurant you can imagine, and he loves using them. Want to go to Perkins? He has a coupon. Red Lobster? Coupon. The only place he doesn't have a coupon for is our house and we hope that Mr. Smith enjoys eating there with us as much as we enjoy having him, even without a coupon.

Wendy Fox was one of Margie's oldest and closest friends. Her parents, Sol and Thelma and her stepmother Margie, zichronam livracha, were long-time friends of Harold and Mickey's.

Judy Dunn

Margie was everything you want a friend to be.

She was kind; she always had a smile and nice things to say.

She was loving; she took everyone under her wing and made each person feel special.

She had a big heart; even when things looked bad for her, she made sure everyone was taken care of and had a seat at the table.

She was fun; everyone wanted to be with Margie … whatever she was doing.

Margie and I played sports together, visited museums, travelled, and just sat and talked. It has been more than 30 years, but I remember vividly lots of laughs, tears, and happiness. She made me a much better person and friend.

Thank you, Margie!

Judy Dunn became friendly with Margie when Margie moved to Washington D.C. where they lived in the same apartment complex. They took many trips together around the country.

Plaque for Margie's Garden at Herzl Camp

Harold Smith, Businessman

Don Mains

Tradehome Shoes began in 1921 with its first store in Superior, Wisconsin, and up through the 1960s its stores were in downtown locations throughout Minnesota, Wisconsin, Iowa and the Dakotas. Today Tradehome Shoes has 109 stores spread across 21 states, from Orem, UT and Boise, ID to Lubbock, TX to Louisville, KY. For well over 30 years, the business was run jointly by Harold and his brother-in-law Don Mains.

I'VE KNOWN HAROLD SMITH for 75 years, first as the young man who dated, then married my older sister Mickey, and then as my business partner of 50 years at Tradehome Shoes.

Harold and Mickey were married in 1943 and Harold came to work for my dad (his father-in-law), Al Mains, in 1946. I came on board in 1950. Al had founded Tradehome in 1921 together with his brother-in-law (my mother's brother) Cecil Ginsberg. After Al's semi-retirement in the mid-60s, Harold and I were the operating officers. We always worked well as a team.

Tradehome grew from nine stores in 1950 to a 65-store chain when we both retired in 1999, selling the business to a group of key employees, all of whom had come up through the ranks at Tradehome.

Through the years, we faced many challenges, including stiff competition from much larger retail shoe operations. Harold played a key role in charting the business through these troubled waters:

- We looked for locations in small towns throughout the Upper Midwest, where there was somewhat less competition.
- We scoured the market, looking for desirable sources for merchandise to appeal to our customers.
- When discount stores came on the scene, we upgraded our product mix to set us apart.
- We recognized the need to shift to imports, which were taking over from domestic sources.
- Harold was quick to see the necessity to add branded athletic footwear to the product mix.
- We made a special effort early on to sign leases in shopping centers as they took over the retail scene.

But the most important factor in Tradehome's success was the quality of the sales organization. We constantly did all we could to train salespeople who recognized that nothing was more important than service to our customers. As Harold so often put it, "We must have a slavish devotion to customer service." This is the not-so-secret weapon that set Tradehome apart from the competition.

Those giant competitors from earlier years, Kinney, Thom McAn, Endicott Johnson, Gallenkamp, Baker's and others are no longer in business. They all failed to recognize, as Harold did, that customer service can be the difference between success and failure.

Harold's life-long love of Judaism and the Jewish people was much in evidence when we traveled together, visiting our stores and going to shoe shows. On these occasions he gave me quite an education in Jewish history, telling me for example about the history of the first Jewish ghetto in Venice or the role of the "Court Jew" in medieval times.

In the days before imports took over the shoe business, we did business with quite a few Jewish-owned domestic factories. Many sales representatives were also Jewish. Harold enjoyed talking with them about how they or their parents came to America, why they settled where they did, how they got into the shoe business, and what their Jewish background was. Their stories always fascinated him, learning for example that the uncle of one shoe factory owner was the eminent rabbi known as Chazon

Ish (Rabbi Avraham Karelitz). Harold often said that he found much in common with these fellow Jews and many became good friends.

Harold and Mickey travelled to many countries overseas and always sought out synagogues, museums and other places of Jewish interest. He shared with enthusiasm what he had seen and learned, and it was obvious how much he treasured these experiences.

Harold and Mickey were so very proud of their Jewish heritage and have given so generously of their time and financial support to the Jewish causes and institutions they loved, among them the Hadassah Hospital in Israel, Herzl Camp, Beth Jacob Congregation, the Talmud Torah, the University of Minnesota Hillel and the Harold and Mickey Gallery for Jewish Arts and Culture at the Minneapolis Institute of Art.

In his business and personal live, Harold lived Hillel's maxim: "If I am not for myself, who will be for me. If I am only for myself, what am I?"

What a remarkable person Harold Smith is! 100 years is just the start of the road to 120!!

Tradehome Shoe store in Mankato, 1951

There are two principles that guide me. The only constant in life is change and the future belongs to those who can manage change. There are self-evident truths that have been tested in the crucible of time.

The success of our company has been rooted in managing change and being completely focused on our core value – providing good value in footwear to our customers. I want to speak briefly about our company history ...

Our emphasis was always on our people and service to our customers. It is no accident that every one of our key executives and managers have been promoted from within the organization. All are native to the Midwest, rooted in the Tradehome philosophy, and hard working to produce the results with which we are all so proud – 75 years of successful service to our customers!

I am proud to be associated with and be part of this success story, which is made possible only by the energy and enthusiasm of all of you!

From a speech given by Harold at the Tradehome Shoes 1996 Annual Meeting

A Celebration of Two Minnesota Institutions

Sri Zaheer, Ph. D.

ONE HUNDRED YEARS! Harold Smith is celebrating a milestone that not many achieve. He is a 1938 graduate of our school, and we are proud to call him one of our own. Harold having made his mark in the world as a Twin Cities businessman, we like to think that we helped him on his way.

In 2019, we celebrate 100 years of our existence. In July 1919, the University of Minnesota launched its business school, now known as the Carlson School of Management. Since the beginning, through Harold's time as a student, and continuing to today, the formula for a successful business school program was relatively clear: match high-quality students with high-quality faculty and house them in a high-quality facility. The higher the quality, the more successful we all become.

Our graduates, from Harold's day down to the present, know that the successful business climate in Twin Cities and throughout the state is due in large part to our program. With the headquarters of 17 *Fortune* 500 companies nearby, we consider ourselves fortunate. The relationships we have built with these high-profile companies, and with countless others, have paid dividends in both directions, so much so that the lines between who is supporting who quickly dissolve. Consider our Enterprise programs. In these programs, student teams work on real-world projects for real companies. The end result is our students receive hands-on, applicable skills and our client companies come away with actionable recommendations. We both win.

These hands-on experiences offer a considerable enhancement to our students' learning experience. Today's students are active learners – they learn by doing, they need to go deeper and broader by working on these real-life, high-impact projects. To do this well, business schools like ours have to be more flexible and have to reach out across disciplines and sectors to coalesce industry with academics. We think of business as our classroom.

We see this mindset of higher expectations in our students from the very beginning. Today's freshmen are coming into four-year business schools with a good idea of where they want their careers to lead. They have often been exposed to entrepreneurial opportunities even as high schoolers. And experiential learning is fundamental to entrepreneurship.

When it comes to entrepreneurial activities, our curriculum is designed to introduce and apply critical competencies while providing the opportunity for students to experience the process of new venture creation. In our Entrepreneurship in Action course, students conceive, launch, and operate real businesses. And no discussion on entrepreneurship is complete without mentioning the school-sponsored Minnesota Cup, the annual competition featuring the best and brightest business ideas in the state. Vying for thousands of dollars in prize money, participants have a chance to see their business plans take root, grow, and hopefully have a legacy equal to Harold's Tradehome Shoes.

Since Harold's time as a student, there have been many other changes in the business school curriculum – among them international learning, dual-degree programs, "soft skills" education, alternative classroom formats – the list is robust and always changing. One aspect that hasn't changed since Harold was at the Business School is the extent to which students benefit from financial support in the form of scholarships, allowing them to take on less debt and focus more on their studies.

To this end, we are pleased to award a one-year, $2,500 scholarship to a Carlson School undergraduate student in Harold's name to honor his robust legacy as a business leader and mentor. And, whatever new trends arise, our promise to students will be the same one made to Harold years ago: the best business education we can provide to meet their needs. Building upon and maintaining these needs are a guarantee that the business education scene will remain highly dynamic for years to come.

Happy Birthday Harold and congratulations for having represented the Carlson School of Management with distinction and honor!

Sri Zaheer, Ph.D., is the Dean of the Carlson School of Management at the University of Minnesota where she is also the Elmer L. Andersen Chair in Global Corporate Responsibility.

Being honored by the U of M Marching Band
Homecoming, 2015

With University of Minnesota President Eric Kaler at TCF Stadium

Sefirat Ha'Omer: On Counting and on Making It Count

Rabbi Mitchell Smith

Teach us to number our days, that we may acquire a heart of wisdom.   Psalms 90:12

Why are our days numbered, and not, say, lettered?
                                    Woody Allen

When you enter the land which I am giving you and you reap its harvest, you shall bring the first sheaf (omer) *of your (barley) harvest to the priest. He shall wave the sheaf before the Lord … on the day after the festival …*

You shall count from the day following the day of rest, from the day of your bringing the omer *(sheaf) of the wave-offering, seven complete weeks shall be (counted); you shall count fifty days to the day following the seventh week, fifty days shall you count …*

And (on the fiftieth day) you shall bring from your settlements two loaves of (wheat) bread, as first fruits for the Lord.
                                    Leviticus 23: 11-17

ACCORDING TO TRADITION, the counting of the *omer*, beginning on the second night of Passover and concluding fifty days later with the

Festival of Shavuot, links the liberation of the Israelites from Egyptian bondage to the giving of the Torah at Mount Sinai. Yet neither in the passage from Leviticus noted above referring to Shavuot nor in the mention of Shavuot in Deuteronomy 16:9-12 is any connection made between the festival and the giving of the Torah; only its agricultural associations are noted. Scholars consider this connection between Shavuot and Sinai to have been asserted at a later date by rabbinic leaders in a time when the Temple no longer stood. With no place to bring the festival sacrifices, the rabbis wanted to keep the holiday central and offered this tie-in. In any case, drawing connections between these two festivals, Passover and Shavuot, made central in our minds by the counting of the days between them, offers some instructive insights.

Shavuot (literally Feast of Weeks) is the only holiday in the Bible that did not have a fixed date; its observance was slated for the day after the completion of the counting of the *omer*, i.e., the 50th day after the *omer* offering (a sheaf of grain) was brought to the Temple. This period eventually became known as the time of *sefirat ha'omer* – the counting of the *omer*. And the ritual of counting the days and weeks of the *omer* became ordained for each night of this period.

As noted, the verses cited in Leviticus present the link between Passover, the time of the barley harvest, and Shavuot, the Festival of the First Fruits, as a strictly agricultural connection. This lent to the *omer* period two nearly opposite facets: on the one hand, it was a time of looking forward to the harvest and to offering thanks for the bounty to come. On the other hand, it was a period of anxiety, as day after day the farmers would check their ripening wheat with the knowledge that some unwelcome act of nature could spell disaster.

In his book *Festivals of the Jewish Year: A Modern Interpretation and Guide*, the distinguished scholar Theodor Herzl Gaster noted the "universal custom of regarding the days or weeks preceding the harvest as a time when the ... life of the community is, so to speak, in eclipse, one lease of it now drawing to a close and the next being not yet assured." It was in this frame of mind that the farmer counted the days to the anticipated harvest.

Uncertainty and anticipation

In athletic competition the element of uncertainty figures quite centrally. A fateful collision in a race, a fall or injury, the putt that missed by just inches – whether competing for professional purposes, glory, or simply as a worthy culmination of months and years of relentless training, success for the athlete can be as meaningful as the successful and bountiful harvest for the farmer. The farmer's counting and anticipation is mirrored in the pre-competition planning, the rituals and the superstitions which the athlete entertains for the similar purpose of staving off anxiety in facing the uncontrollable. Even with the most thorough preparation, the athlete knows that he or she enters the domain of the uncertain.

Facing the possibility of random events over which we have no control, we sometimes turn to ritual and superstition in a quest for some sense of certainty. Hoping to safeguard themselves against unwanted mishaps, athletes make use of rituals and practices intended to bring some measure of control over fate, whether it be the free throw shooter who crosses himself before shooting (not likely to be among the readers of this volume), the linebacker who eats the same meal before each game, or the infielder who takes pains to drive to the stadium by the same route for every game. Baseball Hall of Famer Wade Boggs, although not Jewish, would trace the Hebrew word *chai* (life) in the dirt each time he came to bat. Such rituals and practices help the athlete put a lid on his/her pre-competition anxiety.

It is very human to register an awareness of anticipation – of looking ahead – whether it is to the coming harvest for which one has sowed, and nurtured, and watched over the crops, or to the competition for which one has trained and planned. And if we have rituals to formalize these endeavors, we are less likely to be taken over by the anxiety which is, in any case, present.

With the destruction of the Temple and no altar to which the *omer* or subsequent first fruit offerings could be brought, an association was eventually made between the Festival of Shavuot and the non-agricultural episode of the giving of the Torah. The counting of the fifty days from the outset of the harvest until its conclusion was replaced by a connection between the Exodus from Egypt and the encounter at Sinai 50 days later. A people who had been *avadim le-Pharaoh*, slaves to Pharaoh, became, instead *avadim la-Shem,* servants of the Lord. (Note the play on the word עבד *eved* (plural *avadim*) which means both slave and one who serves, just as עבודה *avodah* can refer both to physical labor and worship/service.)

The liberation became not only a cause for celebration, but a prelude to new restrictions – the discipline of Torah. And through that discipline, a nation of slaves was transformed into a holy people. The call to holiness through discipline is one response to that uncertainty which life imposes.

How do you get to Carnegie Hall?

Discipline, of course, is at the heart of any successful athletic pursuit. Consider current Golden State Warriors Head Coach Steve Kerr, whose string of four straight three-pointers helped the San Antonio Spurs come back from a 15 point fourth-quarter deficit to defeat Dallas in Game 6 of the Western Conference Finals and go on to win the 2003 NBA Title. For Kerr, a perennial reserve player, those were practically his only minutes in the entire playoff season that year. Kerr had previously made the shot that clinched the 1997 title for the Chicago Bulls. Afterwards he told a reporter, "There's no doubt in my mind that the reason I made that shot is because I've practiced that very shot tens of thousands of times in my years of basketball. Doing something over and over and over again gives you the confidence to succeed when the pressure is on."

In a variation of the well-known joke in which a tourist in New York asks a local, "How do you get to Carnegie Hall?" one-time Orlando Magic sharpshooter Pat Garrity was asked the secret to his own three-point shooting prowess. "There's no secret," Garrity replied. "It's lots of practice. The first thing is you have to master the fundamentals of a good shot, and then after you get good fundamentals down it's just repetition and more repetition."

The words of the *Sh'ma* offer similar instruction. Often translated as "You shall *teach them diligently* to your children" (Deuteronomy 6:7), the Hebrew word ושננתם (*v'shinantam*) – from the root ש-ן (*shin, nun*), meaning *tooth*, and ש-נ-ן (*shin, nun, nun*), which the Alkalai Hebrew-English Dictionary defines as "to sharpen, repeat, recite, teach instruct, inculcate," conveys the sense of *sharpening* the teachings of the Torah by constant repetition – "at home, on the road, at bed time and upon rising." In other words, it is a teaching to be engaged in daily, and repeatedly.

Rabbi Michael Strassfeld notes in *The Jewish Holidays: A Guide and Commentary*, "(The covenant at) Sinai is the answer to the question: For what purpose were the Israelites freed from Egypt?" A rabbinic *midrash* (interpretation) explains that great anticipation is the foundation for counting the days from Passover to Shavuot, as if to say, "Each day brings us one day closer to the receiving of the Torah."

Each day potentially brings one closer to one's goals, but one must put forth the requisite effort.

Early in the 2002-2003 NBA season, while struggling with an ankle injury, Hal of Famer Reggie Miller of the Indiana Pacers asked to return to the active roster. Miller talked about feeling a sense of urgency, saying, "I'll worry about the ankle later." Without deadlines our goals lose their essential quality of being compelling. Having a sense of urgency about our goals serves to motivate us to get from "here" to "there."

Similarly, the counting of the *omer* is a ritual that helps us register in a mindful way the importance of the journey from "here" to "there." Whether linking the onset of the harvest to its culmination, or the liberation from bondage to the covenantal experience at Sinai, the importance of counting the *omer* is not simply in recording the passing of the days, but in noting the *meaning* that links the two events, and the link between effort and results. By bringing to the ritual of the *omer* the qualities of anticipation, hope, focus, and intensity, we link the simple act of counting to life's endeavors that really count.

Excerpted from *Baseballs, Basketballs and Matzah Balls: What Sports Can Teach Us About the Jewish Holidays... and Vice Versa* © 2009 by Rabbi Mitchell Smith

This Too Shall Pass

Few of us live our lives free of adversity, challenges and disappointments. Two thousand years ago, a philosopher named Philo Judaeus who lived in Alexandria Egypt, wrote: "It rarely happens that God allows a man to run life's race from start to finish without stumbling or falling, and to escape fouls by rushing past them with a sudden and violent burst of speed."

The following parable offers some solace for such moments, and perhaps a valuable perspective to those of us who, unlike the technologically savvy young, find themselves frustrated when their computers and iPhones won't do what they are supposed to.

IN THE COURT of King Solomon served a loyal officer named Joseph, who took upon himself any task that was required to minister to his master. Often, he could be heard bragging to others, "There is no assignment the king could ask of me that I would be unable to fulfill."

When word of this reached the king, he thought to put the braggart Joseph to the test. He decided to ask Joseph to fetch him an item that did not exist! Summoning Joseph to the royal chambers, King Solomon said to him: "There is a ring that I have had my heart set on owning for some time. It is a special ring that can make a sad person happy, and yet make a happy person sad. I want you to find this ring and bring it back to me in time for the Sukkot Festival, which is six months from now."

Joseph accepted his assignment eagerly. He set off to visit the camel traders, certain that in their journeys across the deserts, one of them would have surely come across such a ring. But, alas, none of them had knowledge of such a treasure. So he turned to the seafarers, hoping that in their voyages to far off lands, one of them might have knowledge of this fantastic ring. But none of them were of any help to him, either.

So Joseph decided that he would have to go off in search of this special ring himself. He traveled from country to country, from bazaar to bazaar, but nowhere was he able to find the ring he had been asked to locate. Nevertheless, the knowledge that his king depended on him to fulfill this mission kept him devoted to the task.

Month followed month, and after Joseph's searches brought him no success, he feared that he might be unable to procure the item he had assured King Solomon that he would bring him. Joseph set forth for yet another country, yet another bazaar, and yet another jeweler's stall. There he found a young lad, and asked him, as he had so many others, if he knew perhaps of a ring such as the one he had been assigned to bring back. Hoping against hope that the lad might offer encouraging words, he learned that the boy knew of no such ring. Deeply disappointed by the news, and with the six months coming to a rapid close, Joseph turned to leave the shop when the boy's grandfather, who had overheard the conversation, came forth and said, "I know of such a ring that truly has the power to make a sad man happy, and make a happy man sad. Wait here and I shall produce it for you."

As Joseph waited with great anticipation, the old man went into the back room of his shop, took a simple gold band, and inscribed something on the inside of the ring. This he then brought it out to Joseph.

Joseph examined the ring, smiled, and said, "Yes, this is certainly the ring I have been looking for!"

Upon his return to Jerusalem, Joseph proceeded to the palace. When the king asked if Joseph had succeeded in his task, imagine his shock when Joseph replied that indeed, he had located the ring as requested of him.

He handed the ring to the king. As Solomon examined it, a strange expression came over his face, for he was reminded that both his greatest accomplishments and his deepest sorrows were but fleeting occurrences.

"Yes," said Solomon, "this is truly a ring that has the power to make a sad man happy and a happy man sad." For what was written on the ring were the words: THIS, TOO, SHALL PASS.

The king put the ring on and wore it from that day forward. And every time he felt sad or depressed, he would look at the ring, whereupon his mood would change, and good cheer would come to him.

Rebounding from Adversity

Rabbi Mitchell Smith

What man who has wrestled in the Game of Life has ever escaped without being thrown or tripped? For whom does not Misfortune lie in wait, like a wrestler who has drawn a bye, taking a breathing space and collecting her strength, so that she can grapple with him at once and sweep him off his feet before he has had the time to regroup for the struggle?

Philo Judaeus of Alexandria

For you have faced adversity, both divine and human, and have prevailed.

Genesis 32:29

A NUMBER OF years ago, the late Israeli Supreme Court Justice Haim Coahen was the featured guest on Israeli TV's version of the popular 1950s television program *This is Your Life*. In the course of the evening, Cohen, a *hiloni* (secular) Jew, described his Orthodox upbringing in pre-World War II Germany. He recounted how one summer day he had shown up at school with several days' growth of beard. (Then, as now, German schools had notably short summer vacations.) It happened to be during the period prior to the Ninth of Av (Tisha B'Av) when Orthodox males don't shave. When the (non-Jewish) teacher of the public school commented on Cohen's somewhat unkempt appearance, the youngster explained that he was in mourning. The teacher assumed that Cohen meant he was mourning the recent loss of a loved one, expressed his sympathies and asked who it was that had passed away.

"No one died," replied the young Haim. "I'm mourning the destruction of the Temple."

"The destruction of the Temple?" repeated the instructor. "I don't recall seeing anything about that in the papers. When did it happen?"

"About two thousand years ago," Cohen told his bewildered teacher.

Indeed, some may find it strange that Jews should hold onto memories of events that occurred so long ago. But for Jews, such memory is practically built into our DNA.

According to tradition, both the First and Second Temples were destroyed on the ninth day of the Hebrew month of Av – the first by the Babylonians in 586 BCE, and the second by the Romans in 70 CE. For countless generations, Jews have marked the ninth of Av with prayers and fasting.

But with the re-birth of the State of Israel, and the fact that most Jews no longer retain hopes to see the Temple re-built, many wonder: why bother anymore with a day of mourning for the lost Temple?

For one thing, remembering such tragedies may well be one of the keys to our survival as a people. Recalling ancient events serves to forge firm bonds with the past. Even if we don't give it conscious thought, consider, for example, the custom of breaking the glass under the *huppah* (marriage canopy). It is done in memory of the destruction of the Temple, tying each individual couple to the fortunes of our people, and reminding us that even in joy we hold an awareness of life's sad side. Distinguished Holocaust survivor and Nobel Prize Laureate Eli Wiesel has stated that, "Most peoples recall their victories. The Jews are unique in remembering their defeats."

But perhaps there is a more compelling reason to recall such events.

We should not forget that the underlying message of Judaism is one of optimism and of eternal hope. While the salt water on the Seder table at Passover serves as a reminder of the many tears that Jews have shed down through the centuries, the Seder ceremony itself concludes on a note of optimism ("Next year in Jerusalem!") bidding us to find ways to face adversity and make of it an occasion to move forward. And while our almost unparalleled trait of remembering tragedies both ancient and modern is a key factor in our survival as a people, no less vital has been our ability to put the past behind us and to rebound from tragedy. On Tisha B'Av we read the Book of Lamentations, a dirge to the destruction of Jerusalem. But on the first Sabbath thereafter, we read from the Book of

Isaiah, where the prophet offers God's words of consolation: "Be comforted, be comforted, my people...." (Isaiah 40:1)

Surely we all look to get through life unscathed. Who in their right mind would ever choose to be visited by adversity? Yet many who have faced it conclude that it enhanced their lives. It is the jolt that takes us out of our comfort zone, jarring the soul, but bringing with it self-examination and transformation.

Veteran actor Kirk Douglas wrote about his own medical affliction in *My Stroke of Luck*. Overwhelmed at first by his situation and deeply depressed, Douglas found his way forward with the help of friends and family. "My stroke," he wrote, "has taught me to be more compassionate, to work harder at relationships with my loved ones, to value friendships more, to be aware of the world around me, to slow down and to have a richer spiritual life ... My stroke taught me so much, and for all that it stole, it gave me even more."

In life, we all occasionally get knocked down. But some people get up more readily than others. And some are even like the giant Antaeus of Greek mythology, who, each time thrown to the ground by Hercules, came back stronger than before. Bonnie St. John, silver medal winner in downhill skiing in the 1984 Paralympic Games, related an important lesson that she learned at the time. "In my first run of the slalom, I was ahead, but then I fell down and had to get up to complete the race. In fact, the woman who won the gold medal also fell down. I knew from previous races that I could ski faster than her. But what won the gold medal for her was that she got up faster than I did after falling down. I learned that everybody falls down, but Olympic athletes get up faster, and gold medalists get up the fastest of all."

Jewish history has no lack of misfortunes which have befallen our people, moments where we have been knocked down and been challenged to get back up. Consider how two such events, occurring early on in the life of the Jewish people, are not only central to our historic memory, but also demonstrate how, under circumstances of adversity, Judaism not only bounced back, but evolved into a more meaningful and more vital entity than before.

The enslavement of the Israelites in Egypt is remembered each year by the *maror* (bitter herbs) of which we partake at the Seder. The Torah tells us that the Egyptians "embittered the lives of the Israelites with harsh labor … and all sorts of tasks they imposed upon them" and that the Lord had "heard their outcry and took note of their sufferings." (Exodus 1: 13-14; 2:24)

The Torah informs us that Israel's enslavement in Egypt was actually part of God's plan, as prophesied to Abraham. (Genesis 15:13) In *The Torah: A Modern Commentary*, Rabbi Gunther Plaut writes: "The Torah … shows God knowingly sending His children into Egypt and subsequent oppression. The Biblical authors offer no explanation why this should have been so, (but it may be that) in Canaan the people of Israel could not or would not become what they were destined to be. In Canaan lurked the dangers of intermingling and absorption; in (Egypt) there would be isolation and segregation, both of which would provide fertile soil for the development of particular national characteristics. If oppression, too, would be part of the experience, this would be the price the people-to-be would have to pay."

Another trauma that befell the Jewish people, as earlier noted, was the destruction (on two different occasions) of the Temple and the exile of our people from their land. This catastrophe, too, may have held the seeds of national regeneration on a higher plane. According to an account found in the Talmudic volume *Avot d'Rabbi Natan*, Rabbi Joshua, a sage who had witnessed the splendor of the (Second) Temple while it stood in Jerusalem, burst into tears one day as he saw the Temple's charred remains. He cried in despair, "Alas for us! The place which atoned for the sins of Israel now lies in ruins." Then his teacher, Rabbi Yohanan Ben Zakkai, spoke to him these words of comfort: "Do not grieve, my son. There is another way to atone besides the Service of the Temple. And what is it? It is deeds of love and kindness *(gemillut hasadim)*, as it is said *(Hosea 6:6)* 'For I delight in kindness and not in sacrifice, says the Lord.'"

While tragedies have left their scars on the Jewish psyche, the Jewish people have ultimately responded to them with both resolve and creativity. With the (First) Temple destroyed and no place to bring the sacrificial offerings, the exiled Jews in Babylonia turned to communal prayer as another way to seek God's presence, a practice from which evolved the worship service which still brings us together in synagogues around the world. The sacrificial ritual of the Temple *(avodah shel Beit HaMikdash)* was replaced by *avodah she'balev*, the offering of the heart. With the demise of the priestly sacrifice altogether following the destruction of the Second Temple, the role of the synagogue, the emphasis on learning and on *gemillut hasadim* came to the forefront, as Jewish practices adapted to new conditions.

No one would deliberately choose to experience defeat and destruction, but perhaps like Kirk Douglas, the Jewish people found some measure of luck in their own misfortune. Had the Jews continued to exist untouched by adversity, we might have gone the way of other ancient peoples. But forced to adapt to the harsh realities which fate dealt them, the Jewish people re-examined and re-fashioned their core beliefs, finding new approaches to Jewish life which not only contributed to the survival of Judaism for the next 2,500 years, but gave birth to noble ideas and practices which the Jewish civilization has bestowed upon all of humanity.

Excerpted from *Baseballs, Basketballs and Matzah Balls: What Sports Can Teach Us About the Jewish Holidays... and Vice Versa* © 2009 by Rabbi Mitchell Smith

As you ramble on through life, Brother,
Whatever be your goal,
Keep your eye upon the doughnut,
And not upon the hole.

-Margaret Atwood

Printed in the United States
By Bookmasters